A Life's Work

ISBN: 9798324634551

Imprint: Independently published

Copyright 2024, Andrew Baughen

All views expressed in this book are those of the author and are not intended for use as a definitive guide. This work is owned in full by the author, Andrew Baughen. No part of this publication may be reproduced or transmitted in any form whatsoever without the written permission of Andrew Baughen: info@soulfulenterprise.org.

This book was produced in collaboration with Write Business Results Limited. For more information on their business book, blog and podcast services, please visit www.writebusinessresults.com or contact the team via info@writebusinessresults.com.

Scripture quotations taken from The Holy Bible, New International Version® NIV®. Copyright © 1973, 1978, 1984, 2011 by Biblica, Inc. Used with permission. All rights reserved worldwide.

WRITE BUSINESS RESULTS

A Life's Work

How to find meaningful
value in everyday work

ANDREW BAUGHEN

ACKNOWLEDGEMENTS

In the beginning, there was an idea that was in its infancy, in need of clarity and applicability. Then value was added as I shared my thoughts and was inspired by other people's insights. They shone more light on the topic and gave depth to the logic and substance to the principles. Gradually, as people added their perspectives, the whole view of value became clear. My lasting thanks go to all those people.

During the process of writing, I've talked to countless people, conducted multiple interviews, symposia and workshops, and read or watched numerous articles, blogs, books and talks. My thanks go to each of those people – many of whom won't know yet the impact their comments and encouragements had on me and the value they gave to me. I hope to thank many of you in person, but for now I want to highlight some memorable examples.

I am amazed by all the Useful Value given to me: Thank you to Chris Stewart for following up with me when I had a bunch of vague thoughts and supporting me with amazingly generous funding to develop these ideas. Thank you to Richard Turnbull for constantly encouraging me that the research was worth continuing.

I am delighted by the Beautiful Value shared with me: Thank you to Arthur Vergani for creating beautiful designs for the WholeValue tools and diagrams. Thank you to Christopher Acheson for helping me turn a jumble of words into a logical form and keeping me on a valuable message as you watched me slowly rewrite.

Acknowledgements

I am grateful for the Individual Value invested in me: Thank you in the early days to Angus Hislop for believing in me and offering me a job that was beyond what I deserved, and to Nigel Taverner for teaching me to say "so what". Thank you in more recent times to my friends at Bayes Business School – to Robert Legget for the connection, to Steve Thomas for taking a risk on me as an EMBA student, to Cliff Oswick for helping form the theoretical model and to André Spicer for enabling the research to continue.

I am touched by the Relational Value modelled to me: Thank you to James Pollard and Yo-Hahn Low for being friends through thick and thin, and to Ajaz Ahmed for teaching me to delight in generosity and settle for nothing less than inspirational beauty. Thank you to Jane Adshead-Grant for showing a gracious human-centred approach to leadership.

I am thankful for the Communal Value that's impacted me: Thank you to Steve Beck for inspiring me to lead an integrated life with a grateful heart for all the value we receive and can offer. Thank you to Elizabeth Corley for consistently taking time to listen and encouraging me to continue making an impact.

I am moved by the Generational Value shown to me: Thank you to my dad for constantly supporting and loving me, and modelling a life of purpose. Thank you to Charlotte and Harriet for being wonderful daughters who live lives of creativity and generosity with great joy.

To Rachel, Charlotte,
Harriet, Max and Spencer –
you are of eternal value and loved
with unconditional grace.

Contents

FOREWORD: MONEY, MORALS AND MEANING	11
PREFACE: CLARITY ON WHAT MATTERS	15

Why we need to know our work has value — 19

We are made to be of value	21
Sometimes we miss the full value	22
Let's reset our view of value	25

How we gain a greater vision of value — 29

STAGE 1: The yes please perspective	31
STAGE 2: The re-evaluating epiphany	33
STAGE 3: The pie baking priority	37
THE VALUE CONVERSATION: ROWAN	*43*

Whole Value — 49

The three lenses of Whole Value	50
The six focal points of Whole Value	56

Useful Value — 69

STEP 1: Identify the useful function	79
STEP 2: Distil your useful contribution	86
STEP 3: Enjoy your useful expression	92
THE VALUE CONVERSATION: TAMARA	*101*

Beautiful Value — 107

STEP 1: Push the boundaries	114
STEP 2: Delight the heart	121
STEP 3: Speak to the soul	129
THE VALUE CONVERSATION: NIA	*140*

Individual Value — **147**
- STEP 1: Grow in stature — 154
- STEP 2: Refine with others — 164
- STEP 3: Seek lasting treasure — 173
  - *THE VALUE CONVERSATION: DAN* — *184*

Relational Value — **189**
- STEP 1: Make teamwork — 198
- STEP 2: Build relationships on values — 207
- STEP 3: Infuse relationships with grace — 217
  - *THE VALUE CONVERSATION: LAUREN* — *225*

Communal Value — **233**
- STEP 1: Shape culture — 240
- STEP 2: Repair and restore — 249
- STEP 3: See, care, act — 259
  - *THE VALUE CONVERSATION: DAVID* — *268*

Generational Value — **277**
- STEP 1: Think as a steward — 282
- STEP 2: Add capacity — 290
- STEP 3: Leave a legacy — 296
  - *THE VALUE CONVERSATION: HELEN* — *303*

Value for Life — **309**
- BELIEF 1: I know who I am — 311
- BELIEF 2: I know what I'm here for — 315
- BELIEF 3: I know where I'm going — 318
  - ABOUT THE AUTHOR — 323

FOREWORD
Money, morals and meaning

Ajaz Ahmed is the founder and CEO of digital innovation agency AKQA, co-author of Velocity, *author of* Limitless *and the founder of the ajaz.org grant-giving charitable organisation.*

Many of the most intelligent and insightful people I've ever met have been those in corporate finance. Yet despite their diverse interests and backgrounds, and regardless of the vast range of companies they lead, there is one blind spot many of them share. When you ask about their operations' impact on the broader society or environment, they don't see why it's their problem.

It's an understandable response. Building a business is a long, hard struggle, and the temptation to see your only responsibilities as being to shareholders, customers and bank balances is strong. But it's a mistake. You can't build a healthy, sustainable enterprise for the long term by carrying on as though you exist in a vacuum. Yes, success in business demands individual endeavour and effort – but it's also about the networks you build and the friends you make along the way.

When I first met Andrew Baughen over ten years ago, I instantly knew he was not the kind of person who thinks leadership is for lone rangers. That's because he wasn't even in business then, having left a high-flying job in the financial services industry to work as a vicar. That's not the kind of career change you come across every day.

Andrew and I were introduced by a mutual friend who's served as a senior adviser to crown princes and archbishops alike. That friend introduced us because he thought we'd have plenty to talk about and because we were neighbours. Andrew's church, St James Clerkenwell, was just down the road from AKQA's office. We both went to work each day in a part of London where wealthy financiers walked the same streets as homeless people trying to make it through another day – and, more often than not, pretended not to notice them.

When you've voluntarily departed the company of high achievers and big spenders to take up a role which requires you to open your door and your heart to every strata of society – rich and poor, success and "failure" – nobody can accuse you of existing in a bubble. Andrew's appreciation of the bigger picture gave us an instant connection. The fact that he has a photographer's eye for beauty and the kind of expertise in biscuits you can only acquire through countless cups of tea with every social group didn't hurt either. He soon became a close and trusted friend.

One of the messages of this book is that you shouldn't underestimate people, and I was as surprised as anybody when Andrew proved the point by announcing another career shift. He wanted to combine his experience as a money man with his second, as a man of the cloth, to see if he couldn't formulate a third way. A way where the

Foreword

cool business brain and the warm human heart could be fused into a philosophy of doing things differently – or, in his words, a formula for "soulful enterprise".

Since embarking on this latest journey, Andrew has been exploring the possibility of soulful enterprise as a researcher and lecturer at a prestigious London university. He mentors the future in the name of building a better and more thoughtful future climate for leadership. This book is the story of what he's discovered so far.

If successful businesspeople overlook the collaborators and circumstances that made their achievements possible, would-be businesspeople often make the opposite mistake. When they seek out the wisdom of those who've been there and done that, they want answers. Business books, looking to sales success or brand business over actionable, practical advice for others, often give them what they want.

But it isn't what they need. It's a matter of definition that you can't innovate by tracing someone else's footprints. You can't make a difference by doing what's already been done. Your passion is yours alone.

In this book, it's not that Andrew doesn't give you answers – it's just that he frames his advice around a series of pointed questions that zoom in on the crucial things that need to be asked and attended to if you're serious about building or steering a business that counts. It's not always easy to find the value in a business plan or to protect the values of an existing operation. But it's always worth the effort. Because while it's nice to make money, it's priceless to know you've made things change for the better.

PREFACE
Clarity on what matters

Professor André Spicer
Executive Dean of Bayes Business School

A vicar walks into a business school. It sounds like the start of a joke, but it is not. When Andrew joined us at Bayes Business School over a decade ago, it seemed like a strange idea to have a religious official working within a business school. Afterall, we are a secular institution which is designed to train business leaders. We are not a church, or a village or even a university with a religious mission.

Initially people didn't quite know what to make of our own in-house man of faith. He took an Executive MBA, then became a regular part of the life of the school. Andrew provided pastoral support for our students, participated in seminars and eventually taught a course on business ethics. He even hosted a group of scholars at a writing retreat in his church in Clerkenwell. In all these interactions Andrew brought a quiet dignity and insight to debates about business. He asked questions about what really mattered.

While participating in the life of the school, Andrew was also working on a project about value. The idea that you need to add value is one of the most commonly heard clichés in business. But what is less clear is what exactly this value means. Often it is only expressed in monetary terms. However, we know that value is much more than that. In this book Andrew explores this deeper conception of value to values and how business leaders can harness it.

This book will prove useful for a wide range of people. Most importantly it will help people who are struggling with finding their way through their career – whether they are at the start, in the middle or towards the end. The book provides a powerful framework for identifying the value which we can add, how that links with our values and what we can do to ensure these are aligned. The book gives people who are facing a career turning point ways of thinking of the challenges they face which are helpful in moving forward.

The book also provides people leading a team a way to think about their own values and those of their team. It helps to give a way for people working together a way of thinking about what value matters to them individually and collectively. Andrew provided a framework for helping to get a team of people aligned and tapping into their deeper drivers beyond money.

This book also gives senior leaders a unique way of thinking about value. Today many companies are developing ESG strategies, diversity initiatives and showing how they deliver on the UN Sustainable Development Goals. The result is often an alphabet soup of acronyms. Focusing on deeper values gives a way of thinking about the things which really matter. It also gives a clear way of communicating purpose and driving change.

Preface

The final thing this book will do is to change the debate about the purpose of business. For too long we were only focused on shareholder value. Now corporates talk about a range of goals associated with creating value for stakeholders. The problem is this discussion can be confusing and sometimes obscure the important things. Andrew helps to bring clarity by focusing on what matters.

Chapter One

Why we need to know our work has value

"Let's change the world."

How does that make you feel? Excited at the possibilities, interested in discovering how, daunted at the scale of what needs transforming in our world or distracted by the issues of the here and now?

Everyone wants meaningful work and everyone can know meaning in work. Work of impact doesn't need to be reserved for certain social entrepreneur roles and work of significance doesn't need to be the preserve of so-called caring professions. There is value in the everyday work of every person who has purposeful intention to be the difference the world needs.

When the object of change is the whole world, it can seem an unrealistic prospect. The key is knowing the part we can play in changing the world. When we see the full range of possibilities, then we can choose which contributions it will be our personal delight to make.

It's like trying to drive a massive truck full of vital supplies over a weak bridge that won't take the weight. What we need to do is unpack the truck and divide into smaller packages that we then drive across in minivans piece by piece. Breaking that down into manageable pieces makes it a far more reasonable possibility. When we see the piece we can contribute, then we appreciate the valuable part we play in a purpose much bigger than one individual but achievable by the combined efforts of many individuals.

What if we all knew and celebrated the ways we are adding value in our work – whether that be caring for the marginalised or checking financial calculations or constructing a building or coding an app or chatting to someone who is lonely or creating a game-changing device?

What if we knew the difference our work is making and were confident that what we do is significant and important? Wouldn't that get you excited about your work again? Wouldn't that change the world?

Finding the meaningful value of what we do starts with knowing who we are and what we're made for.

Why we need to know our work has value

We are made to be of value

We are made to be of value. When I say we are made to be of value, I use that phrase deliberately – it is part of the way the world works that value needs to be added. We don't live in a world where everyone can purchase valuable products from a store or valuable services from a supplier without that value having been created by someone first. For the value to be offered, it needs to be made, grown, shaped, engineered, transported, served and maintained.

Work is fundamentally good because it is fundamental to who we are and how we thrive together in this world. It's not an evil nuisance that stops us having fun, it's a good necessity that enables fun. We're not just consumers of value, we are also creators of value. Before we can sip cocktails on a deckchair, lots of work is necessary. It doesn't all just grow on trees – even the cocktail pineapples need picking, slicing and placing into a glass. This means that we are at our best when we are generative creatives providing value rather than absorptive sponges.

When I was a teenager, there was a TV show on a Saturday whose whole aim was to get you to switch off your telly and do something useful instead. It was a little self-defeating if your aim was to sell advertising based on viewing figures, but it was a valuable message to a kid like me stuck at home, sitting on a sofa. It got me thinking of possibilities and pushed me to get active and do something with my time rather than just pass the time.

Doing something useful is human shaped because it is a context in which we can experience a multiplication of value – we love it when we're shown generosity and we thrive when we are able to show generosity. Generating value is also an opportunity to express creativity – we delight in producing something that helps others, developing solutions to problems, improving or repairing something or introducing the world to a game-changing idea.

Sometimes the name "creative" is claimed by certain industries or job titles but is actually a description of every person who is generating value in their work and should be a key part of every work role. Generating value in work, whatever that value might be, is a creative endeavour and is part of what it means to be human.

Sometimes we miss the full value

We are made to be of value, but what sort of value are we made to be?

It's easy to miss true value as I learnt when observing my daughter who was far more excited about the packaging of her first birthday gift than the toy inside the box! What becomes scarier is when we continue to mis-value things as adults and value something based on superficial things, such as the shiny exterior rather than its powerful potential for good. We assign value based on the money paid rather than the good produced.

An indicator of our attitude to value is how we answer the question: "what's the value of your firm?" Some people give me a single

Why we need to know our work has value

number that is the financial market's current valuation, but others tell me about the value the firm produces. We need a wholescale mindshift away from seeing that it's all about the money – it's about a lot more!

This money-only thinking has been the prevailing view in business and is still taught as the norm in many business schools. For example, I attended a strategy lecture recently during which the professor boldly stated: *"strategy is all about value creation in order to achieve value capture"*. I sat there thinking: *"is that the only way of seeing strategy?"* Although I'd heard the terms many times before, it suddenly struck me that the term "capture" is quite aggressive. It implies holding someone against their will or gaining territory in a military campaign where the capture is a win to our enemy's loss.

The use of military language in business is rooted in how people went into business having served in the armed forces, especially during the world wars in the first half of the 20th century. People who had cut their leadership teeth in the tooth and claw of war became so-called "captains of industry" that blossomed in peacetime. As a result, the winner-takes-all military mindset prevailed and Michael Porter's book *Competitive Advantage*[1] became the campaign bible.

---

[1] Porter, M.E. (1985) *Competitive advantage. Creating and sustaining superior performance.* The Free Press, New York.

But it doesn't have to be that way! If we switch from a military to an agricultural metaphor we gain a very different vocabulary of value. The agricultural lexicon focuses on planting and nurturing growth – it's generative in its thinking and practice.

The word "generative" describes a community of people involved in a growth process: digging, planting, watering, weeding, pruning and harvesting. What if we saw businesses as gardens? Would that change our sense of responsibility for encouraging value generation through all sorts of activities in addition to and leading up to sales of products?

I started my working life in 1986 as a strategy consultant in the banking industry. It was the year of the "big bang" in the City of London when financial markets were deregulated and, in a rush, large American investment banks bought up some of the traditional British merchant banks – as well as jobbing and broking firms – to create new global powerhouses.

Out went the old oak-panelled offices and in came offices with floor to ceiling windows in modern towers and converted buildings along the River Thames. The sight of a banker with a stripy shirt driving a sports car through the ancient streets of London's Roman city was not unusual, and the champagne culture was seen as a symbol of success. "Greed is good" was more than a strap-line on a movie poster, it was a motto for a whole generation.

Why we need to know our work has value

For me personally, having been surrounded by that culture from day one of working, I assumed it was normal to be "all about the money" and I made it acceptable in my mind by saying "everybody's doing it". But every now and then I realised not everybody was living that way or thinking that way. A chink of light showing another world and another way shone through.

Sometimes that came from being treated by an individual with much more compassion and kindness than I was used to or thought was deserved. I remember, for example, a director seeing through a malicious appraisal given to me by a manager who wanted to bring me down to size – she helped me learn from the experience and ensure I had more intelligence on how I was coming across to senior colleagues.

Often the chink of light came from observing how friends handled money, success and power, and listening to their loving challenge to me. We need that gift of seeing from another perspective and being woken up to a different way of thinking about true value and working with full value.

Let's reset our view of value

What makes you feel valued? I imagine it's when you are appreciated by others, when you know you've made a difference in a situation, when you can measure the impact you've had. So if you are struggling to see the value you are generating or being, how can you change your perspective?

When I tell people I'm investigating the value of our daily work, they often admit that they can't see much value in what they do. In reply, I ask them to describe the wide range of activities involved in their work. I love seeing people come alive as they tell me about individuals they help or complex problems they solve or impact that they contribute to.

Knowing the value of your work helps you multiply the value you add to the world. However, learning the value of our daily activities involves going beyond thinking of value in purely economic production terms or thinking of our value as simply the economic output of our jobs.

Value goes far wider than money. Value of lasting worth is generated as useful products are created, staff developed, systems innovated and lives improved across society for generations to come. Generative value is about the value of everything that gives life, growth and flourishing.

Resetting our vision of value provides a shared language with which to clarify our purpose and lasting impact. As human beings we are all inherently valuable, and it's knowing our value and the value of others that inspires and compels us to be of value in our world. Widening the definition of value beyond financial metrics opens people's eyes to all the types of value they are generating, and that in turn strengthens their vision for how the value they produce connects with the values they believe in.

Why we need to know our work has value

Seeing value more widely also makes our purpose beneficial and attainable. One of the messages prevalent in our culture is that to be significant we need to make our mark on the world and aim to be the change that tips the axis of the universe like some modern-day Greek god. The problem is that building such impossible expectations creates a pressure to deliver which can never be met and therefore will only lead to fear of failure and disappointment. Another issue can be that our hearts become hardened by the pressures of life and the problems we face. This desire to make a difference is at the core of what it means to be human. But we can become critical, cynical and self-absorbed.

So, how do we make significant changes? By every individual knowing how they can impact people's lives in a multitude of ways that contribute to a movement of change. Opening our eyes to wider value restores vision to our hearts and heals a sickness of the soul.

Just like we need to update our computer software every once in a while and get rid of things that are slowing the system down, it's good to get some heart and soul refreshment on a regular basis.

This book will equip you to see how your work makes a valuable difference each day that is worth you getting out of bed for. It acts as a friend who is on your side and wants to help you see the value of your work more comprehensively and clearly, who assures you it's OK to think wider, explore deeper and live fuller lives. It celebrates all the value of our work and investigates what more we can do that generates lasting value.

Chapter Two

How we gain a greater vision of value

At its core, adding value is how we express our humanity – our work makes more but also makes us more. The more we see the value we are generating, the more we will appreciate the value we are being.

In the busyness of everyday work where there are decisions to make, hustles to pursue and targets to hit, we can get very focused on the here and now. But while a single focus can be good for a season, we can also develop a myopia to the bigger issues. When that happens, we fail to appreciate the wider value we are having or fail to evaluate the value we could be adding.

Imagine you're taken into a large room with a vaulted ceiling. Everything is pitch black – apart from one spotlight that is shining on a beautiful jewel, gleaming as the concentrated beam reflects off it. What's your impression of the room and where is your focus? It's all about the jewel.

Now imagine there's a sudden noise and lights turn on from every angle, filling the room with brightness and clarity. What you then see is that the room is full of sparkling jewels, many much bigger and more radiant than the jewel you first saw – which is actually off to one side. What's your impression now of the room and where is your focus? It's of an array of jewels each with a characteristic shape, shade and shine.

It's hard to see without the light and sometimes we don't even know what we cannot see unless someone switches on the lights for us. Light doesn't just remove darkness, it reveals reality. That's what happens when we shine light on our work, we see a full array of value, purpose and priorities.

In business, the focus of value is often on one jewel alone – money. We need therefore to see beyond a pile of cash to a whole world of treasures that our work can multiply and go beyond single-figure valuation to whole-value celebration.

There are three stages in moving from darkness to light, from single focus to panoramic vision:

- **Stage one** is an acceptance that we've not found what we're looking for and a renewed desire for more – the yes please perspective.
- **Stage two** is the courage to challenge the current view and evaluate alternatives – the re-evaluating epiphany.

How we gain a greater vision of value

- **Stage three** is a willingness to take action and move from thinking about seeing more value in theory to seeing more value generated in practice – the pie baking priority.

STAGE 1:
The yes please perspective

The first step is to recognise that value is not a limited resource. Generating value for others does not mean you need to be losing value of your own. This perspective is reflected in a phrase at the heart of a family tradition that I have inherited and passed on to my children: "yes please". This tradition relates to Sunday lunch, although it can also be applied in numerous other situations.

In my family, the exciting moment in a Sunday lunch comes after the main course has been enjoyed and the main event is revealed – the desserts. These were always plural in our house as an array of choices ranging from apple crumble to blueberry cheesecake, from rice pudding to sticky toffee pudding and from ice cream to pavlova were placed on the table. My mum would then ask each person what they would like and we were allowed to answer with a "yes please" that meant receiving a bit of each, saving us having to make a difficult choice and ensuring a bounteous bowl was set before you.

The point about a yes please is that there are many choices on offer. If there had just been apple pie on offer and I said to my mum "I want ice cream", that would have been unreasonably demanding, and if I said "I want the whole pie", that would have been selfishly greedy. But because there were many desserts on offer, having a taste of each was sensibly satisfying. Enjoying the value of our work starts with seeing the array of value our work offers us the opportunity to be generating and then deciding which types of value to concentrate on.

This book outlines an array of value that we can be generating through our work. It suggests that rather than choose between types of value, you can be generating several and in fact that's what makes work joyful and meaningful. The "yes please" view is an alternative to the binary view which sees everything as a trade-off between grabbing more value for managers and shareholders or giving more value to customers or society. "Yes please" says "let's generate value for both!"

You are invited to sit back and take in a wider perspective on the good your work is doing for you and through you for others. I encourage you to approach with a willingness to be encouraged as you see more, celebrate more and seek more for both yourself and others. Let's talk about all the value your work is already producing and all the value you long to create in the future.

Let's say "yes please".

How we gain a greater vision of value

STAGE 2:
The re-evaluating epiphany

When we are living in a world which is not ideal, it's easy for us to start believing that the way things are can't change. We paint business in a negative light and describe people as greedy bankers or fat cat executives and forget that they are human beings who love and are loved. Our perspective gets fixed and we stop being able to see how things could be. When we get tunnel vision, a fresh pair of eyes with a different view of value can see the problems and suggest solutions we had been missing.

It all starts with seeing value in everything, everyone and everywhere. Financial value need not be separated from social or environmental value. Our theory of value should be more than the money we make. Instead, the theory of value I invite you to explore is found in a whole range of activities. The commonly held view of value today doesn't have to be that way.

In the Disney movie *Enchanted*, a princess from two-dimensional cartoon fairy-tale land falls down a well and ends up in the far more complicated "real world" of New York. What she encounters is a very different way of thinking about love, work and life in general. She believes in kindness but when she asks an old man for directions to the fairy castle she is confused when he grabs her tiara and runs away. In response she asks: "Why would you do that?"

Her belief system is based on a confidence in happy ever afters – when she is challenged that "life is complicated" and "we don't even know if we'll get through today" she replies: "but it doesn't have to be". Is that just incredibly naive or powerfully bold? Her basis for challenging what she sees is the alternative world she has seen and experienced. She comes from another world and shows another way.

As well as a fresh pair of eyes, sometimes we can see differently by looking through the eyes of history. Mariana Mazzucato in her book *The Value of Everything* sets out how the term value has been used in various ways with various meanings over time. She argues that until the mid-19th century, the value of something was determined objectively and "tied to the conditions in which those goods and services were produced – including the time needed to produce them"[2] and other factors of production.

It was the rise of the corporation and the global economy which detached the value it costs us to make something from the value we charge others to buy it. What if we reattached intrinsic value to our pricing? What if we defined value on the basis of "whether what it is that is being created is useful"[3] rather than just what the market will take and the customer will pay?

---

2 Mazzucato, M. (2019). *The value of everything: Making and taking in the global economy.* Penguin, London. p.7.

3 Mazzucato, M. (2019) p.6.

How we gain a greater vision of value

The movie *Wonka* gives the origin narrative of a young man who dreams of opening his own chocolate shop full of imagination, beauty, care for people and, of course, plenty of scrumptious chocolate. His ambitions stand in contrast to the incumbent Chocolate Cartel, where corruption is fuelled by greed, who look only to fill their bank accounts and maximise their profits. Willy Wonka dares to challenge the norm and wants instead to fill hearts with joy and maximise the chocolate in our pockets. His distinctive views and actions set him apart.

Sometimes we are compelled to re-evaluate value when a challenging situation forces us to take a fresh view of what we value and what value we are in a position to generate, and for who we are able to generate it. Difficult times help us re-prioritise what is of value and what we can do without. How do challenges provoke fresh views of value as you look in, look around and look out?

The global coronavirus pandemic of 2020 led to a re-evaluation of work. There's been what amounts to a hard stop to many parts of the economy, and with it a pause in many established parts of the workforce. What this has done is bring to the fore certain roles which were previously unsung: low paid jobs in healthcare, social care, logistics, goods production and retail.

In the time BC (before coronavirus), stacking shelves in a grocery store would have been considered low down in people's estimations. But in the midst of the crisis, shop workers were suddenly seen as key workers. People in these roles are now cheered by nations and highly valued by governments. What changed? People's perception of value switched as the real value provided by "ordinary" jobs was seen rather than value being measured by the size of a pay packet.

For example, Laura McLellan is a supermarket worker who described how she felt humbled to be told that she and her team of checkout operators were key workers during the coronavirus pandemic. She said: "I never thought I'd be so proud to sell bread and butter".[4] The key difference wasn't in the work itself during the pandemic but the value people saw in that work.

Sometimes our view is changed by a sudden moment of insight – an epiphany. These revelatory experiences change the way we see things, leading us to think differently and transform how we act. Epiphany moments may not happen every day, and it may not be possible to invoke an epiphany, but we can set the stage within which our readiness to see beyond the ordinary is heightened. A great way to start is to take time out and look at the value we are generating from a different perspective.

Following the 2008 crisis, the senior management of a major UK bank went on an off-site event during which they were shown into a room full of memorabilia from the bank's early years. They were invited to dwell on the intentions of the founders and the nature of

---

4 Brown, A. (2020, April 24). *Coronavirus: "I never thought I'd be so proud to sell bread and butter"*. BBC from https://www.bbc.co.uk/news/uk-scotland-edinburgh-east-fife-52399385.

the customers on whom the business was built. Seeing a different view of business and hearing an alternative backing track for business changed their perspective. Going away and disconnecting for a period of time from the here and now issues enabled them to think again about their future direction and the new story they were wanting to write. What they experienced was more than a learning moment – it was sight restoring.

Value is there in business and in our work, but are we in a position and frame of mind to see its true worth? Value is like art. If you are failing to see it, perhaps you are in the wrong position to properly see it. When you look at it from a different angle or in a different light however, you might notice details you had missed before.

As you reappraise what is of real and lasting value, enjoy the view!

STAGE 3:
The pie baking priority

I love pie – savoury or sweet; meat or fruit; with gravy or custard; hot or cold; filled or top-crust. But I have to say that I always get panicked by the question "how big a slice would you like?" as I'm thinking "how many other pies have you got?" It reminds me of the advertising slogan for the dessert Viennetta: *One slice is never enough*. It has always struck me as a very appropriate motto for life!

In the world of pie, there are three basic attitudes to value:

- **Value Guard:** *Holding on to scarce resources and protecting from risk.*

    Seeing pie as a scarce resource means you are always scared of missing out or not getting as much as others. The problem with fear is that it's a strong overriding emotion. Any joy you might have in what you have is replaced by resentment over what you might have had.

- **Value Grab:** *Competitively wanting to collect everything you can.*

    If you view having pie as a right, it is easy to get competitive. Getting as much pie as possible becomes a game that you want to win at all costs.

- **Value Give-away:** *Serving others and giving what we can.*

    "Have my slice" is the phrase of sacrifice and selfless love. This attitude considers that it is better to give than receive and delights in seeing others built up. The classic example is the loving mother who cares more for her children's needs than her own.

The prevailing logic is that Value Grab and Value Give-away are opposing forces, with the only option being trade-off decisions where both lose out. But it doesn't have to be that way.

My experience as a strategy consultant and then a church pastor has helped me see how the "grab my slice", "greed is good" attitude to business is damaging to the soul and leads to competitive behaviour, dissatisfaction with what we have and a desperate desire for more.

It was when I enrolled on an Executive MBA and studied different approaches to strategy and value creation that I began to realise there's another way of looking at business. With a "yes please" perspective, we can see there is a fourth attitude to value. I saw how you can combine the enthusiasm of the Value Grab view and the compassion of the Value Give view in what I call the Value Generate view of value:

- **Value Generate:** *Creating more value that can be shared with everyone.*

    "Let's go bake a pie" is the generative attitude in the world of pies. In contrast to fear, greed or sacrifice, baking a pie generates more for all. It flips the view of pie on its crust. It turns pie consuming into pie producing, eating into baking and grabbing into generating.

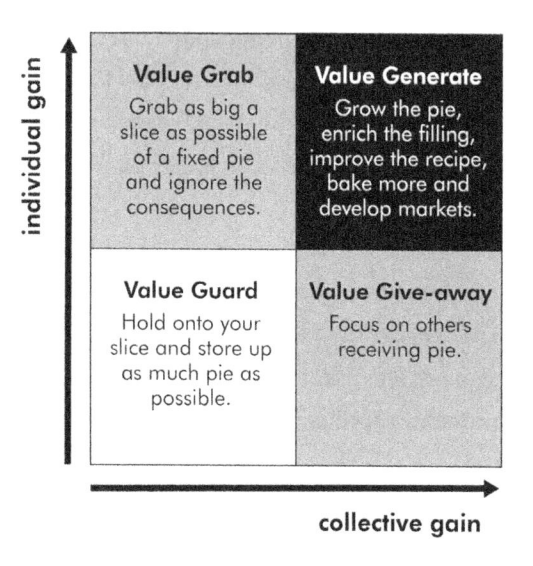

individual gain ↑	**Value Grab** Grab as big a slice as possible of a fixed pie and ignore the consequences.	**Value Generate** Grow the pie, enrich the filling, improve the recipe, bake more and develop markets.
	Value Guard Hold onto your slice and store up as much pie as possible.	**Value Give-away** Focus on others receiving pie.
	→ **collective gain**	

Generating value doesn't just grab for yourself but generates plenty to share with others. It shifts the conversation from "how much money can I make from selling pie?" to "how much value can I generate by baking pie?"

Alex Edmans proposes that organisations can be both financially successful and socially impactful, and therefore deliver both purpose and profit, when they adopt a "pie growing mentality".[5]

---

5 Edmans, A. (2020) *Grow the pie: How great companies deliver both purpose and profit.* Cambridge University Press, Cambridge, UK. p.3.

How we gain a greater vision of value

In his view of business, the pie represents social value and profit is only one slice. But crucially, rather than profit being a bad thing, he sees it as good and necessary (which is a relief considering he is a professor of finance!).

The point is that the pie isn't fixed and therefore we can grow it, and as we do we increase social value and profit – creating shared value enlarges the slices of everyone. He describes how profits grow as social value grows and provides plenty of evidence for this.

Growing a range of value – including social and financial – is the foundation of Value Generate. It sees how the world continually generates growth in all kinds of ways and explores the many different opportunities we are given to multiply the value of what we have. It takes a wider look at all the good that is contributed by the work we do, as well as the cash gained in the process, and shifts the conversation from distribution (pie splitting) to generation (pie baking).

Value Generate also re-evaluates what we mean by value and what we consider valuable. It believes that adding to the world and serving others is the core purpose and fundamental business model of good business, where doing good in business is good for business.

Whatever situation we are in and whatever work we do, whether we have entrepreneur in our job title or not, and whether we work for a social enterprise or a fast-moving consumer goods company, we can all develop as generative entrepreneurs. If I can inspire others to be generating value in their workplaces day by day, then this book on value will have been a book of value!

In the next section we will introduce a method of viewing the Whole Value you have the potential to generate in your work. We will then explore the six main facets of value in detail and suggest practical ways we can be developing the value of what we do and therefore increasing our joy and motivation for doing it.

As you go on this journey of discovery of all the value you can generate, be prepared for a change of heart. We value things we can count on with our heart, not just numbers we can count with our brain.

How we gain a greater vision of value

THE VALUE CONVERSATION: ROWAN
Generating value every day

Rowan is a rising star in his organisation. Having completed his training and gaining his professional qualifications, he threw himself into his work and was promoted to manager. Life was great for Rowan: recently married and living in a newly purchased waterside apartment with all the luxury facilities, he was living the dream.

Yet Rowan still had a question gnawing at him. He couldn't see the value of what he was doing and felt that to feel he was contributing to the world he would need to leave his big firm and join a social enterprise. This wasn't demanded or even expected of him but is what he felt was the only course open to him – he saw it as a choice between achieving the success valued by his contemporaries or doing something valuable with his life.

But does it have to be a choice? Can't we enjoy both?

Yes please!

As we chatted this through we looked at lots of different aspects of his work with clients, team members, groups and networks he participated in, community projects his work sponsored, new technologies he was contributing to and so the list went on. What was clear to me was how disconnected and undervalued many of the valuable things Rowan was doing had become in his mind.

As a result of our conversation, Rowan drew up a plan of what value was important to him and that he wanted to focus on generating, and how he might be able to do that while still working in his current firm. I then recommended he went to his bosses and talked through his thinking and how he wanted to work with them on being even more valuable in multiple ways in the future.

A Life's Work

They responded well to that conversation and have been working with Rowan to harness his vision for value and focus his energies on projects that generate value he believes in. Everybody wins – the firm gets a more motivated and energised employee, and Rowan gets a focus for work that he can see the value of and work to bring value through.

It is so easy to become so focused on a narrow definition of value that you lose sight of the bigger picture and get discouraged. By changing your perspective and stepping back to look at your Whole Value like Rowan, you can not only rediscover the pleasure of doing what you do best, but make a lasting impact on the world and people around you.

Whole Value

Chapter Three

Whole Value

Entire and unbroken.
Complete as nature intended.
All of the goodness enjoyed.

We can all benefit from a switch of view every now and then – whether it's going on holiday and returning refreshed or a new team member joining with new perspectives or reading a book that realigns our thinking or inviting a consultant to give a view. Gaining a wider vision of value provides a compelling purpose for our lives, clarifies what makes our work valuable to the world and prioritises the work we're willing to give our heart and soul to.

The approach to viewing value outlined in this book is called Whole Value. We add "whole" to a word in a wide range of settings, from whole milk to wholemeal biscuits and from wholesale to whole numbers. Referring to something as whole points to its completeness "as nature intended". For example, wholegrain refers to the whole of the wheat kernel that has all its constituent parts of bran, endosperm and germ.

Adding "whole" to the start of a word communicates that none of the goodness is missed by eating the whole apple or speaking the whole truth. In the same way, the Whole Value approach is about looking at the value of our work in its entirety and ensuring no contributions to value are missed out on.

The three lenses of Whole Value

An award-winning photographer explained to me how students are taught photography. The first step is to go out with a camera without taking pictures. The idea is to look through the lens and take in the specific perspective the viewfinder reveals. Next, take some pictures and study what they've captured so that they see all that the camera takes in view rather than just what the photographer was looking at and focusing on. That way, he said, we learn to see the whole story and value every detail.

Whole Value starts by looking through three lenses. For the past 100 years, photographers have carried three camera lenses in their kit bags because the different lenses look with different perspectives which are all needed to see whole. Today's pro smartphones also have three lenses for the same reason – they can't be combined because they are engineered to view in three particular ways.

Whole Value

Each lens has a distinct and necessary purpose:

- The telephoto lens zooms in on specific detail and expands a part of the picture so it can be clearly seen and understood.
- The portrait lens focuses on the people in the picture and blurs out the background so the face pops in the frame.
- The wide-angle lens opens up a wider view so the whole picture can be seen and each part can be viewed in the context of the whole.

Applying the three camera lenses to our work, there are three distinct views of value:

TELEPHOTO	PORTRAIT	WIDE ANGLE
value to customers	value to co-workers	value to wider community

The telephoto view – zooming in on the value of what we make

When we look at our work close up, we can study it in detail. We look at the specific value we produce and provide through our work – both as individuals and as part of the organisations we work for.

It enables us to answer the question "what do you do?" by giving more than a job title and instead giving a picture of value that describes why we do what we do and how it's worth doing with care, skill and effort. So instead of "I'm an engineer", your answer might be "I build bridges that connect communities"; instead of "I'm a delivery driver", your answer might be "I get vital supplies to people".

Some professions such as medicine, teaching and manufacturing have more obvious outputs that have a value which is immediately clear. But it doesn't have to be exclusive to some. Every worker can have the dignity of knowing what they do is of value and worth doing.

Concentrating our view on what we produce takes a closer look at how the things we invest our lives in add value and make a lasting difference. It recognises that when we're on our deathbed we want to be able to say those efforts and hard work were worth it for the value they gave to the world, not just for the value of the stock options we took.

The portrait view – focusing on the value we give to those we work with

The portrait lens brings people's faces into the centre of the frame – both as individuals and also in relationship with others so that each individual is able to make their valuable contribution to the whole. No worker is an island. The portrait lens focuses on the value of working together with others.

People matter and the way we treat people matters. In my research, when people describe the organisation they work for as soulless, I always ask for the practices that cause it. Invariably, the answer relates to people being treated as cogs in a machine. Valuing people with dignity builds valuable organisations of integrity.

The wide-angle view – taking in the valuable impacts our work has in society

As we develop as people, we also develop the capacity to bring value to the world. Growth in value catalyses growth of impact. The more we deliver value to users in communities, the more that value goes on impacting those communities, both in the present and into the future.

The wide-angle lens of value opens up the picture of an organisation's impact on the public good. It shows how value generated by our work continues to ripple out into business ecosystems, local communities and future generations.

All these types of value are necessary and work together to form the ongoing value of our work. That's true for us as individuals and for us together within organisations.

Looking at the Whole Value of Patagonia

Take for example the outdoor apparel firm Patagonia. They are well-known for the impact they have on society in all sorts of ways, but they can only do that by having great products that people want to buy and being a great business that people want to work for. Whole Value is where all facets of value are working together.

In terms of the telephoto lens, Patagonia are at their heart an engineering firm which started out making mountaineering equipment. They are therefore fascinated by how their products perform out on a mountain or in the big surf.

It's because staff use the products that they understand the importance of safety and functionality, and are also interested in how they look and feel – they don't want something that falls apart after two washes or gives way in extreme situations. Quality matters and so does longevity. Patagonia understand that things get torn when scrambling up cliffs and therefore offer a repair service. The clothes are beautifully designed and a pleasure to wear, but the emphasis is definitely on wearing for many years rather than just one fashion season.

When viewed with the portrait lens, the culture of Patagonia comes into view. Having spent some time researching Patagonia, I was struck first by the way a daycare centre for children was in the middle of the office buildings which are on the original site between the beach and a freeway.

Culture is important and staff are encouraged to get out into the great outdoors – people's working hours fit around the tides! The result has been the development of a creative and collaborative culture that creates engaged staff who develop excellent products that grow the business.

And as Patagonia has grown, so has the impact you can see through the wide-angle lens. The commitment to the environment runs through everything Patagonia produces and the firm not only practises better business that is better for the planet, it advocates with customers, suppliers and wider stakeholders. It built its reputation *"as much for its ground-breaking environmental and social practices as for the quality of its clothes"*[6] and was even named the coolest company on the planet by Fortune in 2007.

Valuable companies benefit customers, grow the business and impact the wider world – all at the same time. Generating multiple types of value is a sustainable business model.

---

6   Chouinard, Y. (n.d.). Yale Center for Business and the Environment. From https://cbey.yale.edu/our-community/yvon-chouinard.

The six focal points of Whole Value

Within each of the three lenses there are a pair of contrasting focal points that work together and produce a depth and richness to the picture of value:

- The telephoto lens captures the utility and the beauty of products.
- The portrait lens captures the individual and the relational aspects of valuing people.
- The wide-angle lens captures the present and the future time frames of impact.

The three lenses therefore provide six focal points for viewing Whole Value. Each one adds to the joy of doing something worth doing, and increases our delight at how our work is changing the world:

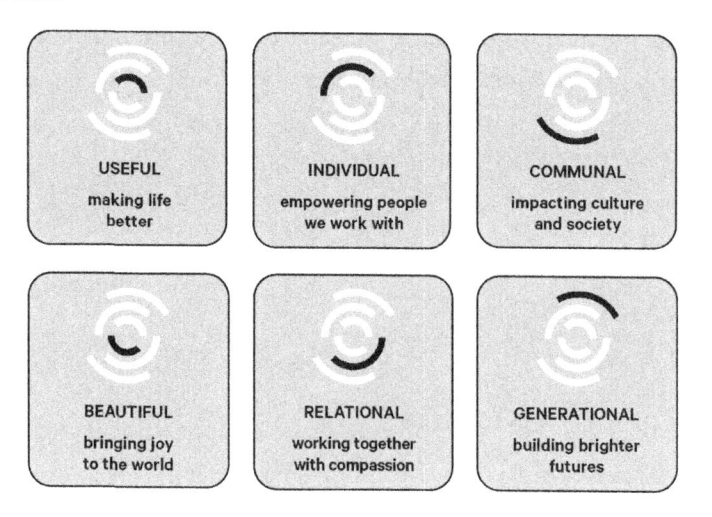

USEFUL	INDIVIDUAL	COMMUNAL
making life better	empowering people we work with	impacting culture and society
BEAUTIFUL	RELATIONAL	GENERATIONAL
bringing joy to the world	working together with compassion	building brighter futures

Whole Value

The six focal points describe the Whole Value generated by organisations and also help us see how we as individuals generate value in a whole range of ways:

USEFUL VALUE

Being beneficial and providing utility to others.
Meeting genuine needs, solving vital problems and building better lives.

Does what you produce in your work make you proud and give you joy? Soulful endeavour comes from creating products and services which solve real problems and satisfy real needs. There's nothing more soulless than doing a task which has no meaning – it dehumanises our sense of meaning and self-esteem.

You can measure Useful Value in the ways the products and services you work on change lives for the better. It might be as simple as a breakfast cereal which equips someone with energy to live and work, or as complex as a laser tool which enables a surgeon to mend a heart.

Providing Useful Value brings us satisfaction as we see how our work deepens the customer experience. This is especially the case when what we provide is distinct from what others can and do offer. It gives joy to know that we are needed and that our value is valued by those who receive it and enjoy it.

A Life's Work

> If someone benefiting from your work sent you a thank-you note for making their life better, what would it say?

BEAUTIFUL VALUE

Lifting the heart and attaining excellence.
Pushing beyond the mundane.

What we produce is valuable when it is useful but is it also beautiful? There is immense value in the daily work of our hands when it is both useful and beautiful. Beauty starts with the way things we make look and work, but then goes deeper into how they make us feel and deeper still as our experience of beauty connects us with the world we long for.

Beauty is seen in the care of design which understands people and brings delight; in enabling people to live full lives; in the joy as a face lights up. It goes beyond useful function and connects with our heart and emotions as well as our mind. It's OK to enjoy things and there's value in bringing joy!

Beauty is also seen in exploring the possibilities and taking people beyond the ordinary to the as-intended rather than as-manipulated; in the authentic truth beneath the airbrushed image; in things being done with excellence and care.

Whole Value

We can assess the beauty of our work by looking at the relational and emotional needs we are satisfying. We can also explore what creative solutions we're known for and how we're adding a "wow" factor that's changing the game. It brings great satisfaction to our work when we act as an artisan with skill and excellence. Our work can shine a light on a better world and invite people to imagine how the world can be.

> If someone said of your work "that's really beautiful", what would they be referring to?

INDIVIDUAL VALUE

Raising people higher in wisdom, skill and confidence.
Enriching with dignity, value and lasting significance.

Each of us as an individual human being are inherently valuable. Nobody is just a number and work gives us opportunities to express who we are and to develop skills and competency. We grow in character through the experiences and opportunities we have at work. We also have the opportunity to develop other individuals with value.

Investing in people because we value who they are rather than just what they can do ennobles them. Parents instinctively know how to bring value to their precious children and help them grow, learn and develop. In the workplace, we have many valuable opportunities to equip people and show them that we care. Developing someone's skill and confidence adds lifelong value.

Ultimately, the value of our work is what it does for us as much as what we do for others. The key is to seek value that lasts, such as love, joy and peace rather than value that minimises us or others, such as control, success or money. Work adds value to us when we gain as people by growing in stature as contributors to society.

> If you asked family and friends how your work has been good for you, what would they say?

RELATIONAL VALUE

Strengthening collaboration, practising generous values, connecting with other stakeholders.
Growing a culture of thriving, promoting mental health, aligning with personal values.

People are not made to be alone and value generation is a collective endeavour. There is something amazing that happens when people work together as a team, looking to the interests of others, acting with humility, showing compassion and cooperating with others towards a common goal.

Like any relationship, we need to work on building our connection with those we work with. As we grow in trust and reliance on each

Whole Value

other we gain from the range of skills and perspectives in the room. There is great value in being challenged by people with very different experiences and insights.

As teams develop and relationships strengthen, there is a generosity towards others that is willing to work through mistakes by giving people a second chance, rather than condemn others – helping everyone to learn and move forward together. There is also compassion towards others that helps those with mental health challenges and grows a culture where all people can thrive. That generosity is also expressed in the way we relate to other stakeholders and how we build a culture as a firm that practises the values it preaches.

> If you brought a dearly loved relative to work, what aspects of the ways you operate would bring him/her joy?

COMMUNAL VALUE

Repairing what is broken, renewing systems, removing injustice, improving outcomes.
Impacting communities, widening inclusion, developing society and shaping wise choices.

A communal kitchen is shared by all those who belong to a community. Common use goes back centuries with the protection of common land, which all can enjoy, and public squares where all can gather. In a world where people are often glued to their "personal devices" and share only with select people, it's good to remember that we are in common with many others and have responsibilities to add in common value as well as benefit from in common value.

When we widen the lens, our outlook on work takes in the value we are adding to society and the impact we are making in the world as the benefits of our work ripple out to more and more people. What we do has consequences, and the more we understand how our work impacts others, the more we can shape that impact in a positive way, and help people live life to the full.

Looking at Communal Value focuses our attention on the social purposes we are contributing to, the problems we are seeking to solve, the brokenness we are able to repair and the injustice we are passionate about resolving. The impact of our work is worth celebrating and it's a delight to see how our actions continue adding value to people, open up access to employment and include in the communal benefits of growth.

It's easy to miss this wider impact that we're having. It's good therefore to ask others what positive influence you are having within the local communities you are part of and the positive difference your work is making to the agencies of society, such as education, the arts, the media, law and government. We don't have to be a social media star to be an influencer – opening markets and following our passion for a just and fair society should get lots of likes!

Whole Value

> If your work disappeared tomorrow, which of your contributions would be missed by local communities and wider society?

GENERATIONAL VALUE

Providing infrastructure, sharing expertise and building capacity for future value.
Stewarding resources, reducing threats and leaving a legacy for the next generation.

One of the most satisfying experiences is seeing people continuing to benefit from something you have created. It makes the hard work worth it and reminds you that value often multiplies with use over time. Generational Value is all about equipping future generations to create value for themselves so that value generation sparked by your contribution continues long after you've gone.

A desire to create Generational Value comes from a hopeful perspective on the future and an understanding that we are custodians for a while, rather than owners and consumers in isolation of the consequences for others. It goes beyond solving an immediate problem by giving people fish to eat and provides for the long-term by teaching people to fish and building up a fishing industry and market. We look to the future by innovating systems used by others and building capacity for the benefit of others.

A Life's Work

Generational Value is shown in the legacy you are passing on to the next generation. That legacy might be resources you have looked after, developed and grown as a steward for a period of time. Our legacy might be in structures built or systems and platforms we've developed. In both cases, Generational Value is an attitude that looks to the interests of others – often people we've not met and will never meet but are delighted to pass on value to. Passing on better requires a willingness to give generously.

> On your deathbed, what aspects of the value you've created will you look back on and say "that was definitely worth the effort"?

Useful Value

Chapter Four

Useful Value

Being beneficial and providing utility to others.
Meeting genuine needs, solving vital problems and building better lives.

If someone asked you "what do you make in a year?" how would you reply? The instinctive response is to give a financial figure. But is money all we generate at work? It could be argued that the only people who genuinely make money professionally work in a mint!

There is a financial value to work of course – we make money by making something worth more to the purchaser than the cost to us of making it. But there is also an inherent value in what our work produces – we make something for the purchaser that enables lives to be lived, value to be enjoyed and more to be generated.

Looking at value through a telephoto lens zooms in on Useful Value and studies how what we do or the products we make serve a purpose and help others. This doesn't have to be world-changing – changing one life at a time through the work we do is still of value.

Many pitch meetings have ended abruptly and many entrepreneurs have seen their dreams shattered in an instant by an investor responding: "You've told me what it is, but can you explain what it does?". It's a simple question that moves from attributes to action and functions to outcomes. Knowing what our work does is vital because, of all the types of value, Useful Value is the most fundamental. An idea has inherent value when it leads to tangible value being generated. Usefulness gives an item purpose and fills it with potential energy.

For example, to say "Google saved my marriage" might be an exaggeration, but its mapping app has certainly relieved a lot of tension on many car journeys. GPS mapping enables anybody to navigate their way through a city and removes the uncertainty people used to have of not being sure when their lunch guests or whatever would arrive.

Now we can track packages, food deliveries and even teenage daughters, and can call ahead and give an accurate ETA to people we are heading to meet. There are clear uses for the product and tangible benefits for the user.

We know what it is to be useful and we also know what it's like to add no value. What do we say when we produce a report that nobody reads or bake a cake that nobody eats? "Well that was a waste of time." A report doesn't have value sitting on a shelf – it only has value if it's read and implemented, or failing that, used to prop open a door perhaps.

Useful Value

Asking about the Useful Value of our work looks at the clear outcomes that contribute to making life better for people and to return to the generative value ideas introduced earlier, it grows the pie. And the good news is that adding Useful Value is not the preserve of a few jobs, professions or organisations.

We are all of value and we can all thrive when doing something useful and of value to the world. I don't need to be saving lives from cancer or rescuing babies from burning buildings to be of Useful Value. Driving a bus that gets people to school or making a boiler that heats water is also necessary and valuable.

Language is important because it shapes our assumptions. Is work just about making a living or is work an inherent part of what it means to be a living human being? Saying "we live for work" minimises what it means to live, but saying "we work because we live" grasps the necessity of work as part of life so that we and others can live.

The search for meaning is an ancient quest. The biblical book of *Ecclesiastes* starts with the narrator, Kohelet, saying: "Meaningless! Meaningless! Utterly meaningless! Everything is meaningless!"[7] The word for meaningless is about being insubstantial and not leaving any mark on the world or any contribution to the world. He then goes on to describe the achievements of his work as "a chasing after wind" which you can never catch and never satisfies. That's

---
7 Ecclesiastes 1:2.

his frustration – he puts his energies and passions into his work but feels that the happiness it gives is fleeting. The answer is the gift of a purpose which makes a lasting difference to people's lives.

It's not just products which need purpose. So do the producers of value. People have an inherent need to be useful and make a valuable contribution through our work – whether paid or unpaid, in the office or the home, for ourselves or for others. Our need to be useful is built into the way we think and is a function of how the world operates. Matter exists in its raw form, but creating Useful Value out of matter requires intentional effort.

Without cultivation, nature runs wild. Without engineers, systems won't operate. Without doctors, patients won't be healed. Without miners, minerals for batteries won't be available. Useful work combines, refines, restores, orders and multiplies. There is a deep sense of satisfaction in bringing that Useful Value into being.

The story I remember hearing as a child, which taught me about the value of work, was of a clergyman walking in a park who stops to look at a flower display and says: "Isn't God's creation marvellous," to which the park-keeper says: "You should have seen it when God had it all to himself!"

But in an increasingly digital age it can be hard to see what all our activity actually produces. I like going to a coffee shop with my notebook and pen to write down my thoughts and create content, but am very aware that I'm the outlier in a room full of people on

Useful Value

their phones and laptops. Technology enables us to create immense value, but when we go paperless we don't get to put our hands on the fruits of our labour and we can get disconnected from the value we are producing in the cloud.

The joy of producing useful work was illustrated to me recently when I visited a glass-making factory while making a documentary. I was struck by the skill and craft of the men and women who worked there, and how at the end of the day they had bowls, jugs and glasses to show for their labour. It made me think about what I would display as the fruits of my work each day. Yes, I've replied to plenty of emails, but what have they actually achieved? Yes, I've read an article or watched a video or gathered data, but what have I actually learnt? We can suffer from the exhaustion of being able to do so much but ending up not feeling like we've done anything! The irony of progress is that we can find it increasingly difficult to track or assess our progress.

When conducting interviews at a media agency, I met Nic who described the issue well:

> *"We have to be very conscious of not just adding to the pile of digital trash. We create things that don't just pop or break the clutter but do so because they provide value, serving some kind of need either known or unknown by the target audience,*

resolving some kind of tension they have or alleviating a pressure".[8]

The combination that Nic describes is important – not just an exciting piece of work that "pops", but value that serves needs; not just adding to digital trash, but alleviating real-world pressures. We are made to be of value and we desire to live lives of value. We want to think that our life counts for something. But the issue comes when we can't see the use of what we're doing, or worse, think our work is a waste of time.

This feeling of frustration is compounded by the pressure on us to be changing the world and making a difference. As an audacious goal it sounds exciting, and we want to be world-changers, but it also feels vast and we can't see how to. Identifying practical usefulness is a way of moving from lofty world-changing ideals to specific value contributions.

We thrive when we are doing something useful and therefore the more purpose we see in something the more power we put into it. Dan Ariely, a behavioural economist, has investigated what gives us meaning in our work by conducting an experiment in which people were asked to build a Lego action figure called a Bionicle.[9]

---

[8] Nic Camacho, AKQA Shanghai Studio, Interview with Andrew Baughen 2019.

[9] *Dan Ariely: What makes us feel good about our work? | TED Talk* (2013, April 10). TED Talks from https://www.ted.com/talks/dan_ariely_what_makes_us_feel_good_about_our_work/transcript.

Useful Value

Each build involved putting together 40 pieces by following written instructions. They were paid per build. After handing each in they were asked whether they were willing to build another, but the amount offered reduced incrementally with each subsequent build. Two groups were tested: designated the "Meaningful" and "Sisyphus" groups. The difference was in how much the work itself was presented as useful and valuable.

For the Meaningful group, the experimenter was sitting behind a desk with many boxes waiting to be built. Each time a subject completed a build, it was displayed on the desk in pride of place in order to promote a sense of achievement and progress for the group of participants. The subject was then offered another box to build if they wanted to keep going.

The other group had the same task but without purpose. The Sisyphus group is named after a man in Greek mythology who is condemned to spend eternity pushing a boulder up a hill, only to have it roll back down and start over whenever he makes any progress.

The experience of the Sisyphus group was similarly pointless. For this group, the experimenter only had two boxes waiting to be built. Once one build was completed and handed in, the subject would be offered the second box. The experimenter would then disassemble the model they had been given and put it back in its box, undoing the subject's work while they built the next. This created a sense of pointlessness, heightened by the increasingly reduced financial reward for each build. The result was that people built 11 Bionicles before giving up in the Meaningful group, and only seven in the Sisyphus group.

Would you put your work in the Meaningful group? The experiment shows that even a small amount of purpose makes a difference to how willing we are to invest in work. Therefore, clarifying the purposeful contributions of our work has the potential to transform our attitudes to our work. We make choices depending on the money we will put in our pockets but we also have the opportunity to assess our work based on the fruitfulness that will fill our hearts.

Clarifying seemingly small amounts of purpose at work can have enormous impact on the energy, care and resilience with which we work. Our work might not be as physical as Lego models, but contributes valuable purposes far beyond the results measured by model building in a laboratory!

Doing something that is meaningless doesn't just waste time, it destroys people. If part of what makes us human is having purpose, then being separated from our purpose minimises us. Standing by and not offering to help when others are struggling at work or in other settings denies who we are, withholds the value we could be and removes the joy we could know. Not being asked to help when we can ignores who we are and can be. Futile work that doesn't make anything robs us of the very purpose we were made for.

Useful Value

Fruitful work makes more and we become more. Doing something useful builds us up and makes us a part of something bigger. You see this in moments of crisis: we have all been in situations where things went wrong and it was "all hands on deck" as everyone mucked in to help out. When that happens, we feel real joy in achieving something of significance – whether that be volunteering to tend and grow organic produce in a community garden or putting up shelves for books in a child's bedroom or getting a spreadsheet to calculate correctly at work.

Adding Useful Value also recognises that our ability to generate value is limited and that we might not be the best person to fulfil what is useful to others. This is an important question when looking at job opportunities. We may meet some or all of the specified requirements, but there is then the need for wisdom as to whether I will thrive in the role or whether someone else would do it better and I could do something else better. The more we know our skills and passions, the easier it is to look at the Whole Value being generated by an organisation and see where we might fit.

Deep down in our being is the desire to do something useful. Having something useful to contribute fills us with hope and a reason to get out of bed in the morning. From the beginning of time, as each day has dawned, people have been driven by the purpose each day of having a part to play in nature's fruitful and multiplying processes that add shape, substance and usefulness.

A Life's Work

> How are you adding Useful Value by contributing to nature's creative processes?

Steps to Useful Value

There is a hierarchy of Useful Value that moves from the practical to the relational and deep down to what value means in our heart and soul:

At the starting level, value is found in the added utility you are providing to users of your services or customers through the work you do.

The middle level, which builds on function, is the added contribution you are making to the range of function available to users and customers. It might be a useful product but identical to others and therefore not contributing distinct or additional value.

But the deepest form of Useful Value is when what we produce is not only useful to the customer in function and contribution but is also an expression of the usefulness we are passionate about providing to others. So, for example, it might be useful for me to provide beefburgers to customers, and it might be that I can do that with a distinct cooking method or restaurant style, but if I'm a vegetarian, it's not a useful type of value I'm going to want to dedicate my life to.

Useful Value

We thrive when we are producing all three, so let's look at each in turn and explore the steps to generating value which has useful function, contribution and expression.

STEP 1:
Identify the useful function

How do you answer when people ask "what do you do?"

It's easy to give a very generic answer which might stop further enquiries in some people, but not in the more inquisitive. The great thing about children is that they keep asking "why?" or "what do you mean?" until they have a satisfactory answer. We could usefully apply that technique to ourselves, and if so, the conversation would go something like this:

> What do you do? I'm a lawyer. Yes but what do you do? I advise clients on legal matters. Yes but what do you do? I remove the worry people have when they make a mistake or someone else wants to do bad things to them.

I was at a pitch event recently where one of the entrepreneurs presented an idea for connecting people who wanted to do work "of impact" in a particular sector with companies making "impact" in that sector. A dating agency for "impact-minded" employees and employers.

But I couldn't help feeling that the whole premise is faulty because it assumes that if we don't have this higher "impact" intelligence, or don't work for a firm making an "impact", then we're wasting our life and will never make a difference in the world. I wanted to scream "STOP" but didn't feel my intervention would be welcomed! But the point is important – do we want to segregate the term "impact" to certain activities or can we show the good and Useful Value of a whole range of jobs, roles and activities?

The way to show the value added by each, and hopefully, every person, starts by looking through the telephoto lens at what our work is adding to the world and the difference it is making to people's lives.

So, for example, rather than a worker telling others that she tightens bolts in an assembly plant, a Useful Value response would be that she makes the wheels secure on the vehiclesthat enable people to travel safely or she helps build scanners that diagnose diseases. Instead of a worker telling others that he makes phone calls in an office building, he could say he listens to people who are having issues with their housing or loan repayments or broadband service and reduces their anxiety by solving their problem.

Focusing our view on the useful function of our work helps us understand in concrete terms what difference we're making and the result is much clearer and stronger motivations for work. It highlights our reason for being and builds satisfaction in a job

Useful Value

worth doing. "Is what you do of value?" should be a question we are able to answer with delight.

The opposite of delight in work that serves a useful function is dismay in work that has futile function. Something can be useless if it serves no functional purpose, such as making an ugly vase that doesn't hold water and tips over if you put anything in it, or building a sign that says "may contain nuts" in the middle of a peanut farm. Something can also be useless if the function we add is not a function customers want.

There is a big difference between products which meet vital needs and those that make no lasting difference to people's lives. For something to have a Useful Value, its function should be clearly measurable because it causes a tangible effect on a person's life – whether that be receiving something they need to live, developing an aspect of their life or giving them the ability to do something. There's not a lot of point in producing something nobody wants, however good an idea it seems to us.

One Saturday morning when I was in my 20s, I was staring out of the window of the office I worked in at all the shiny new cars parked outside. A lot of the cars had the letters GT on the back of the car, indicating that it was a Grand Tour car designed to speed across the countryside and take the driver and passengers on an adventure. The only problem was that the drivers were all stuck in the office for the whole weekend and would take their cars home on Sunday night having seen nothing but a few city streets on a commute to the office.

It was then that I came up with my first startup idea: designer mud. My plan was to offer the reverse of a car wash. Before heading home, busy executives could have their car sprayed with mud so that when they drive up to their door their neighbours can see that they've had an exotic adventure somewhere off-road. I started to research different kinds of mud that could be offered depending where in the country you want to have been in your imagination.

It was all going so well, until I started asking my friends if they'd pay for my fledgling business. I can still hear the roars of laughter. Some ideas don't fly because people don't have enough of a pioneering spirit. Some ideas crash because the pioneer doesn't have a clue what value people actually want. Value needs to have a function that solves a problem or adds benefit.

Useful Value unifies organisations and motivates those who work for organisations. It's far easier to believe in and share in work that serves a useful function. Useful and purpose go together. Inherent within the purpose of any business is the production of products and services with useful purpose. For example, Unilever, the consumer goods multinational, may have a grand purpose to change society, but success in the pursuit of purpose will only be achieved by selling products members of society want to buy and use.

Useful Value

> Do you know and appreciate the value you are producing at work? Is that in line with the vision and purpose you have set and achieving the strategic priorities you are working towards with others?

There are a number of ways of identifying the useful function of what we produce at work.

The Satisfaction Test
Value is generated when a product is produced, distributed and then used. And who is it used by? People. When we forget the people element, our work can become mechanical and instrumental. Adding people in the picture and knowing how our products and services touch their lives gives humanity and compassion to our work, and helps us develop work that is valuable and purposeful.

We may know why we make our products and services, and also know what we say to encourage others to use them, but do we know the reason our customers buy or use our products?

> What satisfaction are people receiving from your work and what would take them beyond "good enough" to "fully satisfied"?

A Life's Work

The Vitamin Test
An important aspect when assessing the useful function of your work is calculating how long the benefit will last. How many episodes of a TV box set can I watch in one sitting before being at capacity? How much more enjoyment do I get from this product over time or are the returns starting to diminish significantly?

Part of understanding how long our work adds Useful Value is knowing whether we are offering a painkiller or a vitamin. Painkillers solve a problem and are therefore an immediate priority. In contrast, vitamins boost benefits and are less of an immediate priority but continue to give in the long term.

Painkillers take away a negative, vitamins add a positive. People buy painkillers with urgency when there is a specific need. People buy vitamins with intentional purpose to build a better future.

> Are you a trainer who is helping people to thrive or a healer who is helping people to live?

The Choice Test
If we're going to serve customers with Useful Value, we need to know their personal preferences. The example given by the

Useful Value

American journalist, John Tierney,[10] is the choice between saving half an hour on your drive to work by paying to use the priority road lane or buying a coffee for your journey. Which choice we make will depend on how urgently we want to get home or how urgently we need caffeine.

For the value we provide to be useful it needs to be a trade-off sufficient people are willing to make. It also needs to be worth us providing in an effective and sustainable way, and within a customer's budget constraints. It may be of value, but is it of sufficient usefulness to prioritise when only some products can be chosen and afforded?

That depends not only on the need our product satisfies, but also the other needs the customer has which are satisfied by others. Our product will be chosen by people when its use compared to other choices is greater than the cost.

Here are some questions that you could use to review the value of each of your products or services to customers who have choices:

- What benefits are gained as it is used or consumed?
- What impact does it bring to people's lives?
- How does it empower further value creation?

---

10 Tierney, J. (Sept. 26, 2004) *The autonomist manifesto (Or, How I learned to stop worrying and love the road)*. The New York Times Magazine.

- What other uses might it have if developed further or something new innovated?

> If you asked yourself "what does your work count for?", what would top your list?

STEP 2:
Distil your useful contribution

For our work to be of value we need to see the problem needing solving and also have the ability to provide a solution. We add the most value where we have the most capacity to be of use. The distinction isn't about willingness to be useful, but about opportunity to make a useful contribution.

It's the difference between my wife asking me to pick up some items from a store on my way home and me saying "can I be of help?" when she is in the middle of a complex spreadsheet calculation. In the first case, I can be of immediate and full value by getting what she needs with no effort required by her. In the second case, I would just add confusion rather than any contribution since my ability is less than hers.

Making a useful contribution in our work often involves going beyond the problem under the problem. During interviews at the creative agency, AKQA, this willingness to peel back the top layer to get at the real problem was identified as a powerful source of value.

Useful Value

Without a proper understanding of the larger objective, they would simply be an easily replaceable vendor rather than an innovative provider of Useful Value.

The surface problem is something generic to lots of organisations and can be solved with a standardised "off-the-shelf" solution. But when we go deeper we realise that the surface problem is being caused by a specific issue related to the particular situation of the organisation. Once we unearth that deep and complex issue we can provide high-value tailored solutions.

Products often have what's called a unique selling point or value proposition. People are a lot more complex than products. As human beings we have a personality and set of gifts, interests and opportunities that is unique to us in space and time. This can be summarised in a personal value proposition (PVP). Our PVP shapes the work we do, the way we invest our time, the people we serve and the projects we are involved in.

The benefits of knowing which specific contribution we can make are highlighted by the example of Tamara and her sports clothing startup (you will learn about her story in more detail at the end of the chapter). Tamara highlighted a particular risk of injury from a type of fitness training, and tailored (literally) a solution that fitted with the lifestyle of her target audience. That enables her business to have a distinct value proposition and a purpose that is adding a fresh and necessary contribution to the world of health and fitness.

The distinct value we offer might be a particular product offering we have capacity to offer or it might be a specialist skill that we are known for. The challenge is to enjoy our distinctiveness when everything around us is conforming to norms, averages of large datasets and predictive algorithms.

Knowing the distinct value you can give is very empowering but not always something society's lenses for value focus on. In a culture where we're taught a set of standardised skills for predetermined job roles it can be hard to promote a particular talent that is part of who we are.

Those things that we offer which are different from others are what make us a great candidate for a job, and yet they are unlikely to feature in a tightly defined person specification for any job selection process. Sometimes it's hard to be different and breaking the mould can be painful, but it's worth finding where you can add particular value.

Knowing what you are best at and doing what you do in the distinct way that you do it is the route to working with purpose and value.

> If you left the organisation you work for tomorrow, what would others miss about your contributions? What does that tell you about the legacy of value you are leaving?

Knowing our PVP helps us see our work with a generative mindset. We look for where we can add most value and we see alternative

Useful Value

providers in a new light. We recognise where others are better placed than us to add value in some situations and therefore invest our energies where we can add most value. It's easy to become so painfully aware of our weaknesses that we lose sight of our strengths or get so carried away by defending against threats that we fail to grasp hold of opportunities.

Other people, both in our workplace or other organisations, are only competitors if we see value in a very monochrome way which misses out on the distinct colour palette of value we bring to the people we serve. When we see that we have advantages in adding value, and alternatives have other advantages we don't have, then we'll experience contentment by keeping our purposeful focus on adding more and more of the value we're good at. Seeing our distinct value releases us from fear and breeds confidence in the value we can be and offer.

Focusing on the distinct and useful contribution we can make also energises us to push our thinking and develop creative solutions rather than just doing how everyone else does it. When we have a mandate to think differently, we gain confidence to push our thinking and brainstorm fresh ideas.

There's something intoxicating about the wild west mentality of going as a pioneer into new markets and discovering new opportunities. It takes what Sionade Robinson calls an Explorer's

Mindset[11] that harnesses bold curiosity, evaluates many scenarios, adopts leading technologies and forms a visionary team who are willing to learn and adapt.

Many entrepreneurs begin with this pioneering vision, but the danger is that they can then get subsumed in the daily details of running and growing a business. Generative entrepreneurs keep the pioneering spirit alive and well as part of a dynamic culture that keeps discovering.

> What distinct contributions are you appreciated for?

There are a number of ways of discovering your distinct contribution.

The Eye Test
When was the last time you looked a customer in the eye and listened to what they think and feel about the services you provide them with? Rather than focusing on the benefits of what you do, as defined by a marketing brainstorm, it is about understanding what actual, realised benefits the user receives.

Distinct value starts by understanding the distinct needs of those you are serving and shaping your work around solving those needs. The value of your useful contribution comes from how the energy

---

11 Robinson, S. (n.d.). An Explorer's Mindset – Senior Leadership Development. Retrieved 5 October 2020, from https://www.anexplorersmindset.com/about.

Useful Value

you put into your product or services transfers to and generates ongoing impact for others.

> What benefits and support are people looking to you for?

The Blue Water Test

Making ourselves usefully invaluable to the people we serve gives our work an extra dimension of meaning and significance. Rather than seeing our exclusive product or service offering as an opportunity to charge super-sized prices, there is joy in a generative attitude that sees our uniquely useful work contributions as a privilege to be handled responsibly.

When we're known for something distinct, we can focus on giving that value, safe in the knowledge that it is wanted by others and can be effectively provided by us. In their book, *Blue Ocean Strategy*, Chan Kim and Renée Mauborgne[12] coin the term "blue ocean" to describe the uncontested water in which a company develops their own unique, distinct position and value.

Applying that to us as individuals, we work in clear blue water when we already have the necessary skills that are prized for the work, but also have that extra something which enables us to offer something in some way that others can't or would find it much harder to than

---

12 Kim, W.C. and Mauborgne, R. (2004) *Blue Ocean Strategy*. Harvard Business Review October p.76-84.

us. It's about following the favour others are showing us and our work, and then finding our happy place, doing work where we can be of most useful service.

> Which of your value-adding activities are necessary and which are a distraction that could usefully be fulfilled by others, if at all?

The Cathedral Test

The story is told of Sir Christopher Wren, architect of St Paul's Cathedral, asking three stonemasons what they were doing. One replied: "I'm cutting stone". The next replied: "I'm earning a living". The third replied: "I'm building a cathedral!" That last reply sees value within the bigger picture. It's when we see how our work fits into a bigger picture that we can understand the distinct value we are contributing to the whole.

> What cathedrals is your work contributing to?

STEP 3:
Enjoy your useful expression

There's a joy in working according to the way we're wired to work rather than feeling an imposter or struggling to keep up. It can be draining and even debilitating doing something that you just know isn't a good fit for you. But the opposite is also true. When we find what we thrive in, we gain energy from it. Even though it's hard and exhausting work, it's also satisfying work that's worth it.

When I was at school, I dreaded gymnastics because I could never get to grips with the most daunting of all apparatus – the high ropes. Most of my classmates could climb to the top like squirrels while I slid off like a slug. But life looked up when we were introduced to the trampoline. Suddenly I was in my element and could freely bounce higher than anyone else in my class – partly because I was a foot taller than anyone else in my class! It became my thing and I gained the nickname Bouncing Baughen!

Just like when we wear clothes that don't fit our size and shape or clothes that jar with our style and personality, we thrive in work that fits us and are drained by the excess energy consumed when we try to do things we're not suited to. Rather than know the joy of being an empowered worker, we can feel like an imposter. The answer is to know why we are the right person in the right position with the right motivation for the tasks set before us.

I had the privilege of being taught about business by some great leaders who set clear examples. One example is Elizabeth, who trained me when I was a 20-something management consultant just starting out in my career. One of Elizabeth's great skills was selecting people for assignments and gathering teams with a mix of skills and experience. I never felt I was an imposter or had no right to be there because Elizabeth made clear that she understood what I could contribute and wanted me to thrive in doing what I do.

I recently met up with Elizabeth 30 years on from when we worked together. She is now Dame Elizabeth Corley, a highly successful business executive, Board Chair and thought leader in the impact investing field. She is also a friend, and I was reflecting with her on the challenges I'm now facing as I pioneer a value-mapping consultancy. She gave two encouragements that had a familiar ring to them. She said everyone, including her, feels like an imposter on occasion, but everyone, including me, can fight that when we work in a field we care about, genuinely want to learn about and have something to contribute to. We are only an imposter if we're pretending to be something we're not or claiming to provide something we can't.

The key to overcoming this "imposter syndrome" is understanding who you are and what your "thing" is – your reason for being and what you are on this planet to do. This could be anything: a combination of talents, a dream you are pursuing or an opportunity you have been privileged to receive. It could be fixed across your life or it might change over the years. Whatever it is, however great or small, temporary or timeless, it's the reason you get out of bed in the morning. It is what shapes the reason why your work is worth doing for you.

If you know what your thing is, it enables you to identify both your skills and the roles in which you are going to thrive. You know yourself well enough that you can assess what you can contribute in any given situation, while maximising your strengths and minimising your weaknesses.

Useful Value

For example, on a sports team, knowing and embracing your "thing" is what might make the difference between being a good player or a great one. A skilled manager will truly get to know their players on a deep level so they can understand exactly how each can contribute best to the greater whole. There are many times a good football player has been moved to a new position that better matches their "thing" and suddenly started to play at another level.

I have seen and listened to people with a lot of unhappiness who have a seemingly great role with all the financial rewards they dreamt of, but in practice haven't found what they were looking for. The concern I have in those conversations is that they never will find what they're looking for if the aim is to prove themselves as a success in other people's eyes.

When our aim is to do something to look good, we will assess our success by how good we look rather than how much good we give. Our work will be consumed by being on the cover of a magazine rather than having an impact in people's lives. Magazines come and go, and being the Person of the Year is rare and short-lived fame. We won't find what we're looking for until we look at the lasting and life-changing value we are equipped to deliver that fits with who we are, what we're good at and where we thrive.

Asking if we should do something is a personal question which gets to the core of our beliefs and values. Deciding whether something is a valuable use of our energies starts with understanding our ambitions and shaping them around the useful contributions we are on this planet to make.

One of my favourite summaries of work ambition is a phrase used by the Apostle Paul who wrote a letter in the first century to the Christians in Thessalonica. They were getting distracted from working and he tells them to get on with their work: "make it your ambition to lead a quiet life: you should mind your own business and work with your hands".[13]

The first part of the sentence in the original Greek literally means "strive not to strive". The point is that we should work hard at not being consumed by a selfish ambition that ultimately consumes our soul and makes us self-centred, competitive machines. Instead, our ambition should be to make a contribution to society and produce something useful by the work of our hands, whether that be handling a hammer or clicking on a keyboard.

By a quiet life he doesn't mean a work-less life but a working life without the noise and friction that harms our wellbeing and damages others. Rather, the route to satisfaction in work is to know our business and mind our business. The phrase "mind your own business" is often used as a criticism, but actually there's a lot of benefit in us being a minder of the business we are called to. It turns work from an activity to a responsibility.

---

13 1 Thessalonians 4:11.

Useful Value

I was speaking to a colleague recently who had received a message from a student he'd taught two years ago. The student was looking back at the impact the lectures had on him and wanted to thank the professor. My colleague, who has achieved a considerable academic reputation and business success, reflected on reading those words: "it doesn't get better than this". The reality is that we are all uniquely shaped individuals and useful work that fits with our gifts, talents and passions will bring life-giving satisfaction.

We thrive at work when we're doing what we're made for and operating with skill and confidence. Like a car in its lane, going in the right direction at a speed that suits it, finding our "thing" at work motivates and brings contentment.

There are a number of ways of discovering our "thing".

The Gallery Test
Discovering "our thing" is shown in what excites us and brings us joy. Work should be fun and getting to know your "thing" is about contributing Useful Value that brings you joy and helps you thrive.

Imagine an art gallery holding a retrospective exhibition of your life. Each picture displayed represents an aspect of value your work has generated. Which pictures would you want people to see first and take centre stage? Which pictures would be less important to you?

Our work can be hard and challenging, but also doing something useful can be a source of joy. Joy can come from the content of what you were doing, the creativity of innovation and new ideas, the community with which you were doing it or the context in which you were doing it.

> What aspects of your work bring you joy and satisfaction?

The Desert Island Test
We get to know our "thing" by looking at our passions, but also by being forced to choose what is really important to us. The classic approach is to imagine you are on a desert island and can only take one playlist of songs, a book and an object. These would then be your only source of entertainment on that desert island while you were stuck there – so pick carefully.

To play that desert island game with your work, ask the question: if you could only keep one aspect of your work, what would it be and why? Use your answers to think through the aspects of your work that are most important to you personally and you would miss if you were no longer able to do them. How can you be doing more of these aspects of work?

> What Useful Value is central to who you are and what you are on this planet for, and a good reason to get out of bed in the morning?

Useful Value

The Quietness Test

Knowing our Useful Value helps us understand how our work makes the world a better place and therefore why we should invest time in it with heart and soul. It gives a quietness of soul that we are in the right place and taking on responsibilities that fit well with us as human beings, and satisfy us with meaning and purpose. It's about moving from seeing work as a job that we escape from on vacation to a role we take on as a vocation.

In the UK government there are Ministers of State who are responsible for the ministry of a department such as Education or the Environment. As a Minister you are accountable for specific work and go to parliament to answer questions and report on that ministry. In the same way every worker has the opportunity of ministry responsibility.

A TV streaming company was struggling with the quality of its sales staff. The normal techniques of targets and bonuses were ineffective and with low customer satisfaction scores. The change came when staff were shown interviews filmed with real customers. Suddenly, the sales teams encountered customers telling their story and they could see their face and emotions as they spoke. They realised customers were all individuals with a narrative to share and needs to resolve. They saw that their "product" wasn't just getting a box ticked, but giving a person value by solving pressing problems such as financial hardship. They grasped the value of their work and discovered their work as a ministry responsibility to serve people and help meet their needs. That gave them more meaningful purpose in their work and a satisfaction in their soul.

Quietness of soul comes from taking responsibility for the business we are to mind without worrying about things outside our ministry portfolio. It changes work from an activity to a calling. It's a great ambition to attain a quietness of soul. It means having a deep peace and contentment in the gift of work and the opportunities work gives to be generous to others.

> How would you complete the sentence "I am the Minister for xxx"? How does that change your attitude to your purpose at work? How does that give a quietness of soul?

Useful Value

THE VALUE CONVERSATION: TAMARA[14]
Clothing that understands sport can hurt

Tamara shares lots in common with many from her millennial generation – loving life and wanting to make a difference. But the dream and reality can be quite different. She described the beginning of her working life as *"consulting in the cloud"* which was *"all about data in a nerdy tech world"*.

It wasn't that Tamara had a problem with cloud computing and she certainly saw its benefits and constantly was a personal beneficiary of the platforms and applications that the cloud makes possible. The issue was more about the fit with what she wanted to do in life and with her life. As she described: *"it just wasn't my bag and I got completely lost in the system"*. I admire Tamara for admitting that when many of her friends were thriving in their work for similar companies that were equally known as caring employers.

When we want to do something useful and there's such a choice open to us as to what that useful contribution can be, it's important to know yourself so that you can choose what fits with you. Tamara was willing to acknowledge the need to make a different choice and courageous enough to step out on a new venture.

Her career pivot was co-founding Blue Elvin, a clothing company producing fitness clothes with a guard that protects the wearer from injury. The specific problem the company is solving is pain and visible bruising from barbell training. People adopting this form of fitness loved what the training did mentally and physically, but getting bashed up on the collarbone, back of the neck and shins became an

---

14 Andrew Baughen interview with Tamara Short 30 March 2021.

inhibiting factor. The result was they avoided training the next day or didn't push themselves and therefore didn't gain the full benefits.

Blue Elvin learnt that 63 per cent of women feared training injuries and that the only other accessories solving this problem are *"quite masculine looking and shouty and we didn't feel there was a brand that spoke to our female consumer in the market"*. It was easy for the founder team to see the value of the product and believe in it.

When I questioned Tamara further on the benefits of the product, she talked about how it empowers people because they're no longer fearful of pain and can reach their potential. It improves technique as you are no longer adjusting your form to avoid pain and also unleashes performance as you can train day by day without bruising.

But there's more to this than technical clothing. Tamara explained to me the concept of "enclothed cognition" which recognises how clothing makes you feel. Minimalist clothes that an athlete wears give you confidence.

The founders of Blue Elvin inhabit the problem they are trying to solve and use the clothes they are producing. There is a passion therefore in the Useful Value that they are generating that comes out in Tamara's words as she explains their driving purpose as a company:

"Women are consistently told to take up less space and be smaller and look a certain way. Their value is often judged on the way that they look. It's relentless, especially for young girls. What we want is to empower women and show them how powerful they can be.

I can't tell you a single female friend who hasn't had a negative relationship with food. That in itself is horrible and such a waste of brain space. You only get one body, why can't we be grateful for the way that it looks? But that's so hard when the media portrays a certain ideal of how you should look.

Useful Value

There's something incredible about being able to lift your body weight above your head. We've found women whose mental health improved as they've become more fascinated about what they can do and achieve. This is not about the way that they look and the aesthetic, it's about what they can do – learning tangible new skills and getting better at their sport.

Exercise is so important and helps give girls confidence and brings transformation. Getting young girls doing this training could be transformative. It could eliminate that horrible five-year journey when you're at school when everybody is trying to avoid PE because they feel very uncomfortable in their own body and are going through all sorts of changes."

Solving a sports injury problem is of immediate value. Giving women confidence and empowering a generation is of lasting value. Through setting up Blue Elvin, Tamara was able to discover a way in which she was uniquely able to provide Useful Value to many by solving both issues at once.

Beautiful Value

Chapter Five

Beautiful Value

*Lifting the heart and attaining excellence.
Pushing beyond the mundane.*

We have looked through the telephoto lens at the Useful Value of what we do. We've seen part of the reason we do what we do is to contribute something useful. Now we are going to look at the other aspect of the telephoto lens – the value of work that is beautiful.

It is often said that beauty is in the eye of the beholder – but is that true? Is all beauty subjective opinion or is there an ideal form of beauty? The queen in the fairy tale of *Snow White* certainly believed in objective beauty but didn't like the information that she received. Perhaps when the queen asked the mirror on the wall who is the most beautiful of them all, the answer should have been that it entirely depends on your definition of beauty.

Are you beautiful whatever people say? The challenge is to have confidence in our understanding of beauty in a world that is constantly trying to tell us we need something else in order to be beautiful. We may sing to ourselves, "what a beautiful world", but there's a whole industry trying to make us think we're not beautiful enough. Countless products, blogs and pages of magazines sell us an ideal that they claim can be attained with the swipe of a card.

This leads to beauty becoming an unattainable vision of beauty at an unaffordable cost. But beauty isn't just a business, it's one of the purposes of business. The beauty of business goes far beyond selling products, it's a way of thinking.

Beauty is a quality that we associate in our mind and senses with emotions of pleasure and joy. These qualities at the surface level focus on form and colour, but beauty is also shown in the quality of creativity and humanity with which things are designed and function, and deeper still are the qualities of beautiful character that give intention and shape the experience.

Deep beauty is seen in the authentic person beneath the airbrushed image; in the joy as a face lights up with interest and compassion; in animated conversation with others; in things being done with care and to completion; in enabling people to live full lives; in releasing joy; in being as intended rather than as manipulated. Beauty is more than a look, it's an action that we can take. There is immense value in work with beauty and of beauty.

In the publishing world, beauty has become a separate genre of books or category of books, or a specific newspaper supplement

Beautiful Value

for weekend reading only – far away from the working week. But beauty can be part of work every week!

Our work has great potential to be of Useful and Beautiful Value – the two are inextricably linked. Beauty and utility are not opposing forces we need to choose between. We are whole people with practical, emotional and, some would say, spiritual needs. The hedonic aspects of pleasure and the practical aspects of survival are both central to life continuing. In fact, it's the combination of utilitarian and hedonic aspects that generate great value.

If my bike was safe and functional for transporting me from A to B, but was ugly to look at and not much fun to ride, it would be useful but boring. If my bike was beautiful to look at and very smooth to ride, but very heavy and slow as a means of transport, it would be beautiful but impractical. I say "what a beauty" when it combines a fun riding experience with an efficient transportation system.

Beauty is at the intersection of form and function. In our work therefore we have the opportunity to do something beautiful, whether we are making something, teaching someone, restoring an object or leading a team. Beauty is an activity all of us can be involved in and is part of the Whole Value that we bring to work and produce at work.

Beauty is an inherent quality in us and in what we make. Beauty is pleasing to the eye, brings joy to the heart and speaks to our soul. Beauty is central to who we are and how we respond to the world around us as human beings, and for that reason should be central to our conversations about the work we do and the value we produce.

This pursuit of beauty isn't a modern invention. In the ancient Genesis account, creation is described as pleasing to the eye and good for food. It is worth noting that the hedonic "pleasing to the eye" precedes the utilitarian functions in God's eyes. Beauty and pleasure is a deeply rooted human need. Part of what makes us more than biological robots is our enjoyment of life and our sensing as well as doing. Work that enlivens us as people has the purpose of utility and the joy of beauty.

The starting point of our desire for beauty is deep set in the human longing for things to be as intended. The opposite of beauty isn't just ugliness, it's anything that detracts what something or someone has the potential to be. So when someone says "that's really beautiful", they are saying that it attains to the perfection and completeness that we long to experience.

As Greg Wilbur puts it: *"despite the rejection of an objective standard of beauty, most people still respond to true beauty"*.[15] For example, people understand the inner ugliness of fear, selfishness and bitterness compared to the inner beauty of peace, selflessness and joy. The pursuit of beauty in our work therefore is any action

---

15 Wilbur, G. (2007) **The beauty of God: Theology and the arts**. Published online October 28 2007. https://www.reformation21.org/articles/the-beauty-of-god-theology-and-the-arts-1.php.

that goes beyond making do to making with delight. Beauty is a pursuit of excellence and of going out of our way to produce something out of the ordinary. Beauty therefore satisfies the worker and serves the customer by producing something that pushes past the mundane.

Our work becomes a soulless endeavour when we are just functional units of production in an organisation which pumps out maximum supply at maximum price with minimum cost. It's very difficult to do what we love when we love beauty, but those calling the shots see income and profit as their first loves.

The danger is that we can start off with beautiful dreams and clear ideals but get lost in the details and the challenges of growth. One of the joys I experience when I run Whole Value workshops for teams is seeing people reconnect with why they got into the business in the first place.

When beauty is seen as an unnecessary cost or added inconvenience then work becomes dull and joyless. When we appreciate afresh the beauty of what our products provide or the beauty of how problems are solved or the beauty of what progress our work is achieving, we are able to refocus and prioritise – refocus on beauty that adds far more value than its cost or prioritise on an ease of use that adds far more delight to users than inconvenience to us.

The problem comes when we introduce beauty to sell stuff and imply delights we're not in a position to deliver. For example, an advert for a car which shows the top-of-the-range model speeding across a mountain pass with the sun shining and everyone smiling is a million miles from the purchaser of a basic model stuck in traffic with the windscreen misting up, the rain leaking through the sunroof and the kids crying in the back. We need to put energy into how our work looks as well as what it does.

Soulful enterprises see the value of combination – beautiful and useful working together – and are more powerful in combination than in their constituent parts. The value of my Apple laptop is that it is beautiful and useful – just on their own neither would bring me much value. A beautifully crafted aluminium enclosure and stunningly clear screen isn't of much use if there are no processors inside to operate anything, and a beautifully designed chip running with more power than you can even imagine is of no use if there's no software to run anything.

You see that interplay of use and beauty in the keynote addresses by Apple executives. They want to emphasise the wow factor of their beautiful products but are also keen to point out how much faster their new products operate or how much more they now enable people to achieve. To be of value we need both.

A Whole Value approach to business sees how value multiplies when utility and beauty work together. But it also recognises that to ensure we look at both fully, these twin aspects first need to be looked at separately. Beautiful Value can't be measured in the same way as Useful Value. If utility is measured in utils, perhaps beauty can be measured in joytils!

Whatever we call the units of measure, there is joy in generating beauty in our work and, once recognised, being able to celebrate Beautiful Value. What joy do you gain from your work? The good news is that working with beauty is always within our control. Once we start thinking about beauty and start asking how we can act with beauty we experience more of the joy of beauty and provide that experience to others.

Steps to Beautiful Value

As with the types of Useful Value explored earlier, there is a hierarchy we can use to study the types of Beautiful Value we have the privilege of generating in our work.

The starting level is the beautiful benefits your work brings that goes beyond the ordinary or utility and is "pleasing to the eye". It's the beauty of work that pushes boundaries of pleasure and makes life happier, brighter and fuller.

The middle level, which goes further beneath the surface, is the way your work is practised with virtues that delight the heart of those it serves. It's the beauty of work that comes from a good heart that seeks to make life kinder, easier and deeper.

But at the deepest level, beauty speaks to our inner being and adds to the satisfaction of our souls. The value we offer people through our work enlivens by making life more beautifully purposeful, gracious and abundant.

Beauty brings great joy to our work when we are producing all three, so let's look at each in turn and explore the steps to generating beautiful and joyful value.

STEP 1:
Push the boundaries

One of the best things my boss did for me when I was learning the craft of being a management consultant was write two words in the margins of documents I prepared. He'd simply ask the question, "so what?" His aim was to push my thinking beyond the obvious and make deeper connections that added insight to the report and value to the client. It has always stuck with me and I'm glad whenever I'm called to think about the "so what?" question.

Beauty comes from a dissatisfaction with something rather bland and from a passion about something more grand. It's a creative energy that thinks beyond the commonplace and keeps going until we've pushed our thinking higher and made discoveries of real beauty.

The pursuit of beauty in our work is any action that goes beyond making do to making with delight. Beauty is going out of our way to produce something out of the ordinary. Beauty therefore satisfies the worker and serves the customer by producing something that pushes past the mundane.

In a culture of pithy soundbites we run the risk of homogenising thinking and saying surface truisms that all merge into one. The most beautiful messages are the ones that stand out and make you think. They are not only clear and concise, they are also deep and developed. Beauty in our work is often the result of developing ideas, iterating and trying things out or gaining other perspectives.

Steve Jobs is well-known for his creative products that "change the game" but he didn't just wake up one morning with the blueprints for an iPhone in his head. Beautiful ideas came from a long and detailed process of learning, trying and discussing. He talked about how it involved people from different disciplines coming together, and he often referred to the power of combining art and science in his thinking, as this quote shows:

> "*My passion has been to build a great company where people were motivated to make great products. Edwin Land of Polaroid talked about the intersection of the humanities and science. I like that intersection. There's something magical about that place. The reason Apple resonates with people is that there's a deep current of humanity in our innovation*".[16]

---

16 Isaacson, W. (2011) **Steve Jobs**. Little, Brown, London. p.53.

There is something very beautiful about creativity with humanity. Human-centric design is the process of creating ideas with the end user in mind. It seeks to satisfy their needs and make life better for them, the utility aspect, and to do that in a way that understands them and makes life happier for them, the beauty aspect. It looks at the real needs of actual users and prioritises solutions that efficiently meet needs with beauty and delight.

Adding beauty to our design thinking drives value by satisfying customer needs, not just solving complex challenges. The result is a user experience that goes beyond satisfaction to delight in the products, seeing how products make life tangibly better, easier and greater. What human-centric aspects of your work and the products your workplace produces connect with people by efficiently satisfying real needs with beauty and delight?

Organisations that adopt the human-centric design approach produce products and services with the beauty of understanding real people and serving real people. As a result, they are firms people can believe in, want to work for and do business with.

Organisations with beauty also pursue excellence. This is a mindset that acknowledges there is potential to develop more beauty in how things are designed and therefore look, work and feel, how things are delivered and therefore are accessible and applicable to people, and also how things are used and therefore are useful to people.

Beautiful Value

Excellence is about pushing thinking to a higher level of what products and services could be and do; it's about not being satisfied with good enough; it's about banging the table (gently) in meetings and encouraging everyone to keep developing solutions; it's about ingenuity in the detail as well as the grand plans; it's about presenting the best version of our products; it's about excellence being a delight.

Sometimes beauty can be hard to describe because it is the combination of many factors which work together and lift from the ordinary to extraordinary. But the good news is that because beauty is multifaceted there are lots of opportunities to improve. Beauty is a process of continual attaining towards an ideal and also an adventure as new technology opens up new opportunities for improvement.

It's a discipline that asks: "how could this be clearer, easier to use and more fruitful and joyful as a result?" It's a habit which is concerned about user feedback not just to improve user ratings but to improve user lives.

When we see beauty as a process rather than just a fixed point of perfection then we look to fulfil potential and see beauty in continual improvement. It's a mindset that asks "how can I make this work more beautiful?" and an attitude to work that asks "what can I do with beauty today?"

There are a number of ways of pushing the boundaries and making beauty a daily practice in our work.

The Caring Profession Test
When I left school for the last time, or so I thought, I went into the summer with an offer to study medicine at a prestigious London medical school. My path was set for many years to come. At the interview I'd been asked the question "why do you want to be a doctor?", and I'd answered confidently by saying: "I want to help people". A life in a caring profession was laid out for me.

Then came an unexpected bump in the road when I got my exam results and missed the grades requirement. After I'd got over the shock I started to regroup, retake some subjects and then got a summer job in a charity in their finance department. The tiny office on an industrial estate seemed a far cry from the caring profession I'd spent my school days dreaming of, if not effectively studying for. But then it hit me.

Helping donors reconcile problems with their payments was also people-centred work. I wanted to help people and I was helping people – just different people than I expected. This realisation led me to study business finance, confident that every profession can be people-centred when a people-perspective is at the heart of the work.

What is the people element of your work? How is the value you add to people something of beauty and worth you celebrating and even developing? Restoring a PPP – a present people perspective – is about reviving our humanity, seeing beyond the walls and becoming people of flesh in a world of living people.

It starts by seeing people and believing that all people matter – they matter to their family, they matter as individuals with talents, purposes, hopes and dreams, and they matter as customers and users that our work serves.

We bring more beauty into our work when we have a people perspective. The Whole Value approach recognises that virtually all work involves people, serves people and affects people. We're all in the people business with the opportunity to add beauty to people's lives.

> Do the people we serve through our work matter to us?

The Kaizen Test

There is beauty in continuously wanting to make improvements. The Japanese discipline of Kaizen is a way of improving standardised processes and practices. The word combines *kai*, which means revision, with *zen*, which means virtue, and is more than a technique – it's a philosophy of change for the better. It certainly fuelled the development of firms such as Toyota who adopted the Kaizen way to great effect and promoted the continuous improvement movement.

Today it's seen in all sorts of areas of business, including high-performing sports teams. For example, the British cycling team demonstrated how lots of small improvements added up to big differences in overall performance and multiple gold medals.

One hundred people improving a process by 0.1 per cent each in theory can add up to 10 per cent overall gain, although in practice the maths of adding performance gains is more complex. But the point is that improving processes and gaining more value from innovations and process technologies is everyone's responsibility and opportunity.

What particular aspects of excellence in your work give you personal pride and satisfaction? Athletes have a goal in mind of a perfect performance. In your work do you have an objective standard of excellence to attain towards?

> How can the Kaizen philosophy be applied in your work?

The Systems Test
Excellence isn't just having the best product possible but the whole process by which the product is brought to market and used to solve problems. There's beauty in the process, not just the result.

There's something very beautiful about systems thinking that takes in all the elements that surround the issue being studied and contributes to the solution suggested and the value therefore generated. And the beautiful truth is that we can all contribute beauty to that process.

Systems thinking harnesses the value of a team approach and joins together global technologies, local expertise, innovations from a range of disciplines and players from a range of sectors into a cooperative system. It recognises that no single person has the full picture and that multiple perspectives on a problem allow fuller analysis of the problem and potential solutions.

> What can you add from your perspective that would contribute to systems thinking in your workplace?

STEP 2:
Delight the heart

Having just received some exciting news, my daughter went into a long client workshop and because she was bursting to tell somebody, she announced at the end of the meeting that she was expecting. As you would expect at such news, people said congratulations. But then something more unexpected happened. Charlotte added that she was expecting identical twins and the client team burst into spontaneous cheers and applause. Why? Because our hearts overflow with joy and delight at such abundant news. When was the last time your work caused someone joy and delight?

Beauty is worth celebrating because beauty lifts our hearts with delight. Beauty enlivens us. We feel delight in beauty that we encounter in a word, attitude or action that gives us life or makes life better.

Beauty may be in the shape and form of the product which is a thing of wonder to behold. Beauty may also be the manner with which a service is delivered that shows a generosity, kindness and truthfulness that gladdens our hearts. Beauty may be in the human-centric design that understands us, works as we'd intuitively want it to and makes life easier straight out of the box.

Beauty starts with the heart because, as we saw earlier, something is beautiful when our senses find pleasure in certain qualities. When our heart is alive to beauty, it delights in qualities that are pure and pleasing. The issue is that we can get overwhelmed by a lack of beauty and become so anxious at the threats we face that we become closed in and just make do. Beauty can become an optional extra rather than a core calling.

This is especially true in a workplace where money and maximising shareholder value takes precedence over everything. Where beauty is shiny gold, or its electronic equivalent, decisions are made based on chasing those shiny things, but can leave us feeling unsatisfied when our hearts long for a deeper beauty and meaningful value. We can become dehumanised when decisions are made purely on what is profitable and adding aspects of beauty to a product is only done if it can be justified in increased sales.

Beautiful Value

When beauty is a means to an end rather than the end in itself, our work contributions also feel like a means to another person's end goal. When that happens, our work can become robbed of beauty and our hearts are starved of joy in beauty. We do what is required to reach a financial target and ignore any thoughts of doing something beautiful beyond what is passable.

Sometimes this is a gradual switch, especially for firms that start with heaps of social purpose and world-changing vision. I have seen many times in my research how the next funding round and the demands of investors for growth and return can narrow vision and the beautiful story of the firm, which is core to its soul, can get sidelined or even forgotten.

But it doesn't have to be that way. Even in a workplace where money is king and beauty is not cherished, we can be bringers of beauty. That can be hard to achieve at the corporate level but is often possible in the tasks we are personally involved in where we have the opportunity to add beauty in both attitude and action.

The difference is about perspective, and it shows in practice – you can tell someone who serves coffee, for example, because they are invested in the coffee shop and get enjoyment from serving, and someone who is just there for the hours they are paid to do the job they are required. Same cup of coffee, very different levels of experience. If you were asked to score their experience from ordinary to beautiful, giving distinct scores would not be hard. Our attitude and actions depend on the story of beauty that we believe.

Which of the following narratives do you think is the reality?

In the beginning, the world was full of beauty, abundance and opportunity. Many people enjoyed all that is good and multiplied more for others. But some acted in selfishness and grabbed more than their share and more than they needed. The destructive actions of a few caused damage and lack for others. But the earth has amazing potential to heal and restore to life and people also have the capacity to act in beauty and do good.

Or:

The world has evolved from a primaeval soup through the processes of natural selection by tooth and claw. Only the strong survive and winning the competition is the only way to get what we want. Ideas of beauty are naive and unnecessary unless it gives me a survival advantage. So I make do, hold fast and ensure nobody stops me doing it my way.

The first narrative is full of hope that even though beauty isn't always seen, the potential for beauty is there and the capacity for beauty is in us. It recognises the problem of greed and selfish behaviours but also accepts responsibility to be a force for good.

The second narrative is full of ambition and thinks about beauty as a useful advantage rather than a posture of the heart. It is driven by personal success and what is good for the individual. It may say "follow your heart" but the emphasis is on the word "your"!

Soulful enterprises follow the first narrative. They want to offer more delight to users and that starts with us delighting in beauty and in the role we can have in bringing our beautiful world back to life.

Is that the narrative your workplace follows and in what ways is that demonstrated? Or in your workplace is there a tendency to believe the second narrative and think of beauty as naive and unnecessary? What causes that de-emphasis on beauty? How could you present another view that promotes beauty in the work you do and the things you produce?

Take time out to appreciate and celebrate the beautiful "it is good" of what you do.

As a minister of a church I've married hundreds of people (to their spouses I hasten to add) and my favourite part is when the bride comes down the aisle and the groom sees her in her dress for the first time. At that moment, is he thinking: "*I've never seen her in that style of dress before, how unusual*"? No! He's thinking: "W*ow! I've never seen her looking so beautiful, how magnificent*".

We love beauty and we respond to beauty. In the same way, our customers and those who benefit from our work love beauty and respond to beauty. In our heart we want more of the good stuff which feeds our soul. I believe that's because beauty is at the heart of who made us and why we were made. As human beings made for beauty and made to make with beauty. Let's enjoy generating beauty and celebrating the beauty we bring into being each day!

There are a number of ways of bringing beauty into our work that delights the heart.

The Artisan Test

Long gone are the days when you were able to go into a cafe and ask for a coffee. Now you have to give specific instructions about the type of bean, variety of milk and additional flavours. You then enjoy the sight of a barista hand-crafting your beverage with skill and care, even adding a picture to the frothy milk as it's poured. The experience is completely different from getting a drink from a machine because the attitude is completely different. The artisan approach is about putting skill, effort and heart into what you do.

To what extent do you work as an artisan? Are there elements of your job that use craft and skill? Beauty shouldn't be the preserve of luxury brands or premium service – beauty can be a normal expectation when we work with the attitude of artisans, expressing our passions and skills with delight.

> How would taking an artisan approach change the way you work and bring more delight to your heart?

Beautiful Value

The Greek Test

The ancient Greek philosophers spoke of three prime virtues: truth, goodness and beauty.[17] Truth is about a perfection of information, goodness is about a maturity of behaviour and beauty is about a fullness of emotion. We can have strength in academic rigour and an ethical lifestyle but lack any delight in beauty. When that happens, our truth becomes lifeless and our goodness becomes graceless.

There's no joy in discovering truth when our heart isn't engaged and we don't appreciate the beauty of our discovery. Similarly, there's no joy in good actions when our heart isn't engaged and we do things out of our duty and adherence to rules, rather than loving the beauty that goodness brings.

Whole Value thinking looks to develop solutions that are infused with an abundance of all three. That way, the product or service doesn't just attract on the glittery surface, but is beautiful to the core and has a beauty in use and in how solutions are experienced. We can all be design creatives as we think about the products and services we are innovating and offering with truth, goodness and beauty.

> How is truth, goodness and beauty infused into the work you do and the way you do it?

---

17 Zahnd, B. (2012) *Beauty will save the world. Rediscovering the allure and mystery of Christianity.* Charisma House.

The Kathy Test

One of the consequences of working from home becoming common practice is that you get to see how your friends are at work when you visit them at their home. I had that experience with my friend Kathy who manages a technical team for a large organisation. She had just ended a meeting and everyone dialled off.

But before Kathy got up and grabbed a coffee, which would have been my next step, she immediately redialled one of the people on the call and asked: *"Why didn't you speak up? I wanted to introduce you so that others could get to know you and see all you have to offer them"*.

A little later that day, when Kathy shared how she felt her work seemed meaningless at times, I reminded her of the extra call she'd made and how beautiful that was. Kathy replied: *"It's because I know how talented he is"*. That's the point – Kathy made the extra call because she cares about the colleague, because there was value there that her team was missing out on and there was value he was missing out on sharing and enjoying.

The beauty of Kathy's attitude of care led to a beautiful action of coaching and that will lead to many beautiful outcomes as the colleague learns to speak up and adds more value to others in the future. I would hazard a guess that Kathy frequently does similarly beautiful things out of her care for others that add value to others without her even knowing she's doing it. There's encouragement in seeing and celebrating beauty at work.

> How are your work attitudes leading to actions and outcomes of beauty?

STEP 3:
Speak to the soul

The way we see value is rooted in the way we see the world and our place in it. We give voice to our view in the language we use and the stories we tell. There is a whole industry that is creating stories about the value of the world in which we live and have our being. Therefore, how we tell those stories and magnify the beauty in the narrative matters.

Ajaz Ahmed, founder and CEO of the creative agency AKQA, is a great storyteller. He makes the point that *"the language of business is changing"*. He describes how the lexicon of words *"used to be efficiency, productivity, profit and growth, but now the words that really matter are purpose, beauty and optimism"*.[18]

---

18 Hlupic, V. (2019) *Humane capital. How to create a management shift to transform performance and profit.* Bloomsbury Business, London. p.89.

Beauty is more than a surface aesthetic, it's an inherent characteristic. As a business embeds beauty into its narrative and uses words such as beauty in its everyday language, it starts pointing to something greater and more wonderful that we can share and experience. Beauty is a quality that lifts our vision beyond the ordinary to the ideal.

The opposite of beauty isn't ugliness, it's anything that detracts from what something or someone has the potential to be. For example, people understand the inner ugliness of fear, selfishness and bitterness compared to the inner beauty of peace, selflessness and joy. Just as smart people can do dumb things, beautiful people can do ugly things.

When that happens we find the dissonance between what is projected and what is practised confusing. It destabilises our view of the world when something as beautiful as a rocket that can be propelled up into the sky is then packed with explosives and targeted to land on a city of people. I have heard the distress experienced by some people who work for companies making amazingly beautiful products but finding the workplace secretive, siloed and soulless.

Our desire for beauty is set deep in human longing. When someone says "that's really beautiful", they are saying that it attains to the perfection and completeness that we long to experience. We may never fully experience complete perfection, or even expect it, but we do accept the concept of it as a reality beyond our current experience. As Greg Wilbur puts it, delight in objective beauty is *"one of the pivotal indications ... of divine disclosure"*.[19]

Beauty speaks to the soul in four ways: correspondence, newness, beyondness and centredness.

1. Correspondence

Deep down we have an emotional need and longing for a beautiful world. When the beauty we experience corresponds to the ideal we hope for, it speaks to our souls. Our beliefs about the world and the values we live by are being confirmed. It verifies that what we fully believe in is demonstrated in reality – perhaps only partially, but manifested nonetheless.

An act of kindness delights our hearts because the beauty we receive corresponds to the reality we seek. Beauty connects us with the ideals we aspire to, makes us more alive and gives energy and meaning to our work. As a result, it inspires us to bring more of that corresponding beauty. Knowing how true beauty elicits delight in the world gives us joyful purpose and motivation that feeds our soul.

Beauty also gives hope that protects our soul. The beauty of sunshine after rain or a new dawn reminds us that no matter what, a new day will come. We need those reminders in our work that a day will dawn after the storms when the sun pokes through again.

---

19 Roy Anker quoted by Greg Wilbur https://www.reformation21.org/articles/the-beauty-of-god- theology-and-the-arts-1.php.

There are so many aspects of work that demonstrate the beauty in harmony, ingenuity and creative artistry. The more we experience beauty that corresponds to the desires of our souls, the more we will be strengthened and assured for every good purpose and beautiful work.

2. Newness

Beauty captures our imagination when it breaks into our current existence with something extraordinary, when it introduces into a challenging situation something new and pure. Elaine Scarry, a professor of aesthetics, describes standing in the presence of beauty: *"The beautiful thing seems – is – incomparable, unprecedented; and that sense of being without precedent conveys a sense of the 'newness' or 'newbornness' of the entire world"*.[20]

When something is unprecedented, it is new to the world or to our experience, and therefore deepens our appreciation of the world and knowing of ourselves. Many products and services claim to be the latest new thing but only a few are unprecedented in the way they cause a seismic event which changes how we view the world and even how we view ourselves.

The ability to fly across the Atlantic gives us unprecedented access to travel. The ability to put telescopes in space gives us unprecedented

---

20 Scarry, E. (1998) *On beauty and being just. The Tanner Lectures on human values.* Delivered at Yale University March 25 and 26, p.16 (https://tannerlectures.utah.edu/_documents/a-to-z/s/scarry00.pdf).

ability to see the universe. The ability to contact people on social media platforms gives unprecedented ability to stay in touch with friends. The ability to perform genetic testing gives unprecedented ability to identify health issues.

Each of these discoveries and innovations adds something new to the world – allowing us to better understand the world we live in, while living safer, healthier and more connected lives. This sense of *"unbornness"*, as Professor Scarry puts it, gives us hope about the future and a reason to work with a delight in the possibilities of newness. Rather than feeling that the outcomes of the past have to be repeated in the future, we can bring in the new.

3. Beyondness

Beauty elicits an emotional response in us and takes us beyond monochrome, utilitarian or purely financial aspects of value. The language of "taking us beyond" is important here as it assumes there is a beyond that we can connect to and want to experience. That vision of the beyond counters a negative view that the world is just getting worse and worse by believing there is a wholly different way that we can experience and work towards.

Tolkien, the author of *The Lord of the Rings*, describes the ability in a genuine fairy story to share a glimpse of "joy beyond the walls of the world":

> *"In such stories when the sudden 'turn' comes we get a piercing glimpse of joy, and heart's desire, that for a moment passes*

A Life's Work

outside the frame, rends indeed the very web of story, and lets a gleam come through".[21]

He uses the illustration of walking down a country lane with a garden wall on one side. As we walk along we see glimpses of a garden beyond the wall – hear the birds tweeting in the trees and smell the blossom. He says those glimpses into a different world are what the great stories of human history teach us – a whole new reality where people are treated with grace rather than conditional performance, and there is a joyful abundance rather than a fearful scarcity.

Tolkien loved to include those glimpses in his stories as he saw how they nourish the heart and soul. In a world of chaos and loss where things can seem out of shape or a shadow of what we hope for, he spoke about a longing in our heart for restoration and reassurance – a world we were made to inhabit where there is a happy ending.

Everybody needs hope in order to do anything and beauty reconnects us with hope. I know I need that reminder on a regular basis. I need regular warnings against becoming hardened and cynical, and constant encouragement to retain a youthful desire that seeks beauty in my work and celebrates gleams of sudden and miraculous grace.

---

21 Tolkien, J.R.R. *On fairy-stories*, Andrew Lang lecture, 8 March 1939.

Our work has the potential to tell a beautiful story that is part of a greater story which involves us and those we are serving. We have the opportunity to serve those who our work is benefiting by letting a gleam of the beautiful world we long to inhabit shine through.

The ugliness of selfishness and the atrophy of brokenness reduce the beauty we experience and lower our expectations. That's why work that adds beauty to people's lives connects them to the way we wish things to be, builds hope that it doesn't have to be this way and motivates them to be part of writing a new story of beauty.

> How does your work point people towards beauty that gives joy and hope?

4. Centredness

When we see and grasp beauty, it reorientates our perspective on our work and our place in the world. Beauty shows us something bigger than ourselves, roots us in a kind of love greater than we can imagine and enables us to experience a purity that is poignant.

This encounter with beauty causes us to see much more value around us and also challenges a self-orientated view with a view that puts us in a wider context. The impact is that others come into view and self is de-centred. As Professor Scarry puts it:

> *"We are standing in a different relation to the world than we were a moment before. It is not that we cease to stand at the*

center of the world, for we never stood there. It is that we cease to stand even at the center of our own world. We willingly cede our ground to the thing that stands before us".[22]

There's something deeply refreshing about encountering beauty – it can be world shifting. When in the presence of something or someone distinctly "other" than us, we reappraise ourselves and our place in the world. It makes us more aware of others and creates a humility and gratitude to be in the world.

> How does your work help people cede ground and recentre?

There are a number of ways of enabling our work to speak to the soul.

The Wow Test

One time, when I was driving along a coastal road in the early evening, I suddenly became aware of being watched – not by one or two nosey people, but by crowds sitting on the bank next to the road. I felt like a racing driver just about to take the chequered flag with adoring fans cheering me on! But I knew they weren't there to see me at all. Their sight was fixed over the road and past the beach to the sun setting on the sea. Thousands of people had come with their refreshments to experience a "wow" moment.

---

22 Scarry, E. (1998) p.77.

Beautiful Value

We have a "wow" moment when we are struck afresh at the beauty of the world and the joy of life. Preparing for that moment of joy involves stepping out of task mode and joining in the value of the moment, the story someone is sharing or the success your team is achieving. We can spend our whole energies doing things or being in transit between things that we never get to stop and enjoy anything!

Sometimes we need to stop and enjoy the wow of the moment. Then we can start to celebrate how far we've come and see with delight what more is to come. How can we do that individually but also with our team?

> How could you create more "wow" moments for you and others to enjoy?

The Reset Test

It's human nature to find joy in the beauty of the world and be motivated by all the potential the world has to offer. It's often called the enthusiasm of youth.

Children are great at enjoying the moment and I imagine I'm not the only parent who has shouted at the children to stop having fun and get in the bath or whatever as they've been told. But that illustrates the danger – we can gradually find our enthusiasm dampened by knockbacks, hostility and toxic attitudes from others. Eventually we lose sight of joy or hope and get starved of anything that feeds our soul. When that happens, and before the hard experiences harden us, we need to reset by encountering beauty afresh.

One of the reasons we love to travel is to experience something outside of the daily routine and immerse ourselves in new places and people, beautiful sights and sounds, exciting food and drink, and enchanting practices and traditions. That's especially true when we go out of our comfort zone in terms of the culture we experience.

The way we respond helps us challenge fixed ideas with something different and compare our assumptions with others that we are now experiencing. Beauty is a powerful way of doing that – especially when the beauty we experience has an unexpected newness to it.

We can encounter beauty afresh by experiencing the new but also by switching off the old. When we travel we also benefit from the process of switching off some of the inputs that we're normally plugged into. Pre mobile phones we were literally unplugged from most forms of communication when we were away from work or phone. You have to go a long way to be out of reach of any communications system, but you still have the power to switch off data roaming on your personal device!

One way to re-encounter beauty is to go on a retreat that practises detachment from the things we treasure and gives the opportunity to reappraise what is really valuable to us and therefore of true beauty. A retreat often involves the process of switching off but also

Beautiful Value

gives space for reading, listening and meditating on the beyondness of beauty that recentres us.

The challenge is to gain from a retreat in order to be able to re-engage at work. We are people who thrive by generating value. We can't do that with beauty if we never take time out to reflect on beauty, but can't do work with beauty if we stay in retreat the whole time!

> How could you get time away for a reset when you can encounter fresh beauty and joy in your work?

A Life's Work

THE VALUE CONVERSATION: NIA
Designing beauty on purpose

"Nia" is a Swahili name that means "purpose" – mechanical engineering graduate Nia Simpson certainly lives up to her name. The more I talked with Nia the more I was struck by her desire to do something purposeful but also something that is beautiful. Nia is full of life and delights in celebrating all the beauty and good purposes life offers.

But it wasn't always the way she saw life or her work. There were times on a placement in a design consultancy where she started to question the value and purpose of some of the products being designed. Then, as she celebrated her 21st birthday, her uncle died. She says[23]:

"It was around that time that I started to ponder a lot. I realised the brevity of life and I started to question 'am I satisfied in what I'm doing? Do I feel I'm adding value? What legacy am I leaving?' Because obviously when someone passes away you think about legacy and I was thinking about his legacy and the mark he made on his family and it made me start thinking 'what is this life and why are we here?' and it really brought me back to considering these things".

She continued in work placements with the feeling that:

"Something isn't quite right here. There's a dissonance between what the company does, what I do in the company and my own values".

This feeling never went away, even when secure job offers were made to her. None of these offers enabled her to provide the Useful and Beautiful Value she felt called to share with others.

---

23 Andrew Baughen interview with Nia Simpson 9 April 2021.

Beautiful Value

The turning point Nia points to was in the penultimate year of graduate studies when she had the opportunity to visit a care home for a product design project. As she interviewed residents for yet another student assignment she describes:

"I didn't expect how much I would enjoy working directly with people, hearing their problems and trying to help them. There was this one moment where we were going in to do some research and just ask questions and we were talking to an elderly lady and she was like 'why are you here?' and I said 'we're here to listen to your problems' and she was kind of blown away and said 'oh wow, nobody's ever done that'. And it was at that moment that I realised that people just value people listening to them and trying to help solve their problems".

When it came to her final year dissertation, the brief that caught Nia's eye was about rethinking the cane used by visually impaired people. In her research she used the user-centred design process that kept the focus on the needs of the user and listening with empathy.

But she still wasn't sure what problem her product would solve until she met a visually impaired person who told Nia how she was nervous about a job interview she had the next day. When Nia asked why, she explained: "as I walk into the interview with my white cane people judge how competent I am on first impressions".

"It was in that moment that it hit me that a tool that's meant to help with mobility and independence can be a hindrance from a social point of view. I felt quite emotional and saw that it's not fair that something meant for good can be not good in certain circumstances. It was seeing her express that stigma that led me to think I want to address this."

Nia came up with an idea that addressed this issue of "stick stigma", and the rest is history. She is now founder of Compact Cane which is a discrete digital mobility aid. The lesson from Nia, purpose in name and in nature, is that getting out of the lab and seeing problems real people face turns a clever idea into a life-changing solution.

Her desire to leave a mark on others as her uncle had, and her delight at helping the elderly who are mostly forgotten by the design world, put her on a track that was receptive to life-changing rather than just money-making briefs. As Nia has progressed in her career she has kept in mind those twin purposes of creating Useful Value and Beautiful Value together.

The lesson from Nia is simple yet profound: The Useful and Beautiful Value you purposefully seek to generate will set the agenda for your life and the value you find in life.

Individual Value

Chapter Six

Individual Value

Raising people higher in wisdom, skill and confidence. Enriching with dignity, value and lasting significance.

Part of why I work is to do something valuable – it's what we see with the telephoto lens that focuses on Useful and Beautiful Value. But I also work because I am someone valuable and I want to express my value in the value I add.

Looking through the portrait lens helps us see our Individual Value – value we develop as unique people. Individual Value recognises that work can be good for us and that the things we do develop us, the challenges we face shape us and the lessons we learn equip us.

Every human being is individually significant. We are people, not numbers. In a world where we can become little more than an IP address with data attached, it's reassuring when we are recognised as individuals and called by name – especially, I find, when they pronounce it correctly!

When my grandchildren were born, the hospital referred to them as "Twin 1" and "Twin 2". But they're not just two of a kind. Even though they are identical genetically, in practice, they are individuals with their own characters and lives. As they've grown, it has been a delight to see how Beatrice and Amelia have grown and developed into people who I can tell apart by the ways they act – even if not by the way they look.

We are all valuable individuals with our own hopes and dreams, perspectives and passions, skills and characteristics. The question is whether we seek to score, standardise or celebrate all the aspects that make us who we are.

When our individual traits and aspects are scored, we are ranked or assigned value based on how useful those traits are considered to be to others. Imagine a conversation with someone at a networking event who is looking to sell their product. This person might assign value based on how they see your worth as a business prospect – if they decide you are not what they need, they will move on to the next conversation immediately.

Standardisation on the other hand fails to scratch past the surface. It looks at points of data like the colour of your hair or scores on exams, while failing to account for your lived experience or the unique and quirky way you might think.

When our worth is based on someone's ability to get what they want from us or a set of standardised metrics, we feel undervalued.

Individual Value

Whereas celebrating and recognising those aspects of us that make us unique and provide our Individual Value is deeply motivational as it demonstrates that we actually matter as people.

We all know that feeling of being treated with value. However, we also have all heard the phrase *"Please hold, your call is very important to us"*, followed by a wait that makes us feel far from a priority. An office wall or company website might proclaim *"We're all about people"*, but that's not always our experience. So, how do I know I matter to someone?

When they notice me, want to spend time with me and invest in me. By relating to me, that person is giving me value and communicating that I'm important to them. Receiving that value builds me up, gives me confidence and shows me where I'm valued and of value.

> Do you feel valued at work? Are you noticed and needed by others or just a replaceable cog in a machine? Are you a number or known by name?

Celebrating Individual Value is important in a society which tends to value so-called celebrities at the expense of other "ordinary" individuals. I recently watched a TV show in which celebrities are filmed at home viewing their television. In this episode, the celebrities were watching a documentary about emergency calls to the ambulance service.

At one point, a boy rang and described how his father wasn't well. The operator quickly diagnosed that the man had stopped breathing and instructed the boy to start heart compressions. There was a long wait as nothing changed, but then suddenly the dad spluttered back to consciousness. The operator stayed calm throughout and at the end said "well done" to the boy before handing over to the ambulance crew when they arrived.

I can't imagine she was paid anything near what the celebrities receive, nor is she celebrated as they are, but she should be. They could only watch from the edge of a sofa with awe as she actively generated value. The skills that operator had developed were the result of hours of training, mentoring and encouragement by the ambulance service – an investment with life-changing results that are definitely worth celebrating.

Who are the celebrities in the workplace? Everyone who applies their skill and talents to generating worthwhile value. Every job has the potential to produce value and every worker should be able to feel valued and valuable.

We are robbed of that value when we start making comparisons with others, especially when those comparisons are based on an imposed measure of value which is more about number of followers or number of zeros on a paycheck. We celebrate our value as individuals when we appreciate our innate value and express that in our life of value.

Individual Value

It's like the difference between a dollar bill and a diamond. The banknote only has whatever value that has been assigned to it – without the promise to give the bearer value, it is just a piece of paper. But a diamond is valuable intrinsically, whether or not it's a diamond in the rough or cut and polished for all to see.

Knowing our value starts by accepting that our value is not externally assigned but is based on our intrinsic worth. We are valuable in and of ourselves.

Like a diamond, this intrinsic value becomes more valuable to others as we refine and shape it. Just like a dull rock becoming a shining jewel, the more we realise and celebrate our intrinsic value while refining and maturing ourselves as individuals, the more impact our value has on the world.

This then becomes a self-fulfilling prophecy – seeing our value and having our value celebrated by others makes it easier and more rewarding to add value in every aspect of our lives. There's an order here that we switch around at our peril.

The anchoring point to a life of value is knowing that *"we are fearfully and wonderfully made"*[24], as the ancient psalmist puts it. We have to know our value and then grow in value so we can give value to others. Otherwise, we risk what I call the "when-then" syndrome.

---

24 Psalm 139:14.

This happens when we believe that when we achieve a particular goal – getting a job or promotion, publishing a paper, building a following – we then will be able to be of value. When this happens, we are scoring and standardising our own value – telling ourselves that only certain people or achievements have value – rather than celebrating the value we intrinsically have.

The issue comes when our value isn't pre-assigned based on who we already are, but based only on what we can do. When we are assigned value as a result of performance, we will either be fearful of falling short or prideful in our superiority. A huge amount of energy is wasted in the workplace figuring out what people think of us and how we're doing compared with others.

Wanting to be the best is a good thing, but working to prove we are the best to our bosses, rather than be the best for those we serve, is going to disorder our motivations and decisions. It's difficult to serve two masters, so what difference does it make if one side is removed and you are already approved of as valued? When we don't need to prove our value, we can be of value without needing anything in return.

The best managers are the ones who equip team members for success and then send them into the field with the words: "I value you and trust you to get on with your work". That value-based commission is very different from the boss who says: "I don't think much of you but go and prove me wrong by getting some work done". Fear might drive us to run from a fire but doesn't help us jump out of bed in the morning and head for work with joy.

If our value is earned by our performance, then we are all in deficit considering how much of the planet's value we have consumed and destroyed. If value is learnt by our reading and philosophy, then why do we have a right to call ourselves more valuable than the chairs we sit on? But the value of people isn't earned or learnt, it's received.

By celebrating the value we already have, we can look to develop that value as a continual process. Just like we need to go to the gym or do some other form of exercise to develop our muscles, living a life of value involves intentional training so we hone our skills and keep learning new ways of contributing.

> How does knowing your intrinsic value as a human being shape what value you create at work, who you are creating it for and why you are motivated to create it anyway?

Steps to Individual Value

As with the types of value explored earlier, there is a hierarchy we can use to study the value we have the privilege of generating as individuals in our work.

At the starting level, we generate value as individuals through our growth in skill, and therefore confidence in our valuable work contributions. Doing good work is good for us and we grow in status as we develop the work we were made for.

The middle level recognises that we work in cooperation with others and develop the value we can offer in relationship with others. We add value as individuals when we add value to other individuals and allow them to add value to us. As we work with others, we all gain more as we are changed by and through each other.

The deepest level is the value we gain as individuals by knowing our place in the world. Work gives dignity and delight. It also gives us a meaningful purpose that gives us delight rather than driving us into the ground. Through work we don't just make more, we become more.

Let's look at each of these three levels in turn and explore the steps to generating value as individuals through work.

STEP 1:
Grow in stature

Let me tell you about two people with similar names and backgrounds but very different work experiences and very different stories of growth and personal progress at work.

Individual Value

Charlotte, or Charlie as she prefers to be called, loves her job. She wakes up on a Monday morning ready to brush off the after-effects of the weekend and jump into the challenges and creative opportunities of work. She grabs a second coffee and goes into the Monday touch-base meeting pleased to be able to chat through projects and issues that need addressing.

She feels able to share and ask for advice, knowing that others will make it their responsibility to help where they can and problem-solve together. Charlie feels valued and is willing to take on new roles and help out in unfamiliar roles as she wants to learn and develop.

In fact, she can look back and see all the ways she has grown in skill and confidence in the past and acknowledges that the tough times were especially formative. She has grown in character and has learnt from mistakes and taken on criticism as learning points. There have been lows as well as highs, but in her mind, the value gained is worth it.

Charles, or Charlie as he prefers to be called, tolerates his job. He wakes up on a Monday morning full of the after-effects of the weekend and goes to work wishing it was Friday. He grabs a second coffee and goes into the Monday touch-base meeting keeping quiet when others talk about their projects and issues that need addressing in case he ends up being asked to do more work.

He feels nervous about being judged and doesn't feel able to share or ask for advice, in case others take advantage of his weakness or claim some of his hoped-for success. Charlie feels like he's a cog in a machine and is unwilling to do more than the minimum to get his paycheck.

In fact, when on the rare occasion he looks back and assesses his work, he sees a lot of disappointments and unmet expectations. He has been criticised for his mistakes and learnt to keep his head down. There have been highs as well as lows, but in his mind, he can't see that work has been a good thing for him and doing less would seem to him to be success.

The example of the two Charlies is replicated in countless organisations. People can be in the same sort of job at the same point in their career and yet have completely different experiences. Why is that? Some reasons will be contextual and about the culture and practices of a particular firm. Other reasons are more internal and about how we respond to culture and practices, what we expect from work and how able we are to learn and develop.

Both Charlies had some experience of that Monday morning feeling but differed on how much they let it affect their mood. Both had a touch-base meeting, but differed in how they engaged with it and what they expected from colleagues in it. Positive Charlie went into her meeting looking for opportunities to make the hard work ahead of her more manageable, while Negative Charlie kept his head down and wished he was doing anything else.

Individual Value

Both had highs and lows, but what they learnt from their experiences and how willing they were to grow and develop was very different.

Positive Charlie sees opportunities to learn, grow and use her creativity to add value and make a difference. Her phrase is: "let's try it and push through this exciting challenge". The other sees hassles rather than opportunities and is resistant to anything that is going to add pressure. His phrase is: "I can think of many reasons why this will be very difficult to achieve and few reasons to make the effort".

The reason our Charlies see opportunities so differently is that their attitudes to learning have contrasting bases:

- Positive Charlie sees that learning comes from every experience we have and especially when things go badly, or we make mistakes. She is willing to take risks, confident that the experiences – whether good or bad – will be instructive and help her grow. She processes experiences and learns more about herself, others and what to do or what not to do in the future.
- Negative Charlie, on the other hand, has less confidence in his Individual Value. Since he assigns himself value on what he can do, a lack of knowledge or skill feels devaluing. This leads to Negative Charlie deflecting criticism by redirecting blame or becoming defensive as a protection against feeling less valuable as a person, rather than looking for opportunities to grow and refine his abilities by learning.

A Life's Work

When you fall into the "when-then" syndrome and assign yourself value based on your performance and what we currently do, this leads to problems. It makes your work more challenging and stressful as it adds pressure to continually prove yourself. When combined with a fear of falling short and failing – a natural part of learning for everyone – you might find yourself in a similar situation to Negative Charlie. His fear of failure, combined with the pressure he places on himself to perform, makes it difficult to adopt a continuous learning model that might help him refine himself and grow in value.

While we have Individual Value intrinsically, a continuous learning model which looks for ways to learn and develop can help you refine yourself – helping raise your stature and ennoble yourself and those around you. "To ennoble" means to change state – when we ennoble, we raise up. Developing people with valuable skills and confidence ennobles them, raising them in stature with greater dignity and depth of character.

Greater dignity and depth of character can't be grown and developed in a vacuum – it's through hard times and adversity that we grow. This means that we need to look towards the value we're gaining, like Positive Charlie, rather than focusing on the value we feel we're missing. After all, learning doesn't just happen in a classroom, it can happen anywhere: from a highly charged meeting room to a pressured deadline on the factory floor. The exciting vision of work is that it can be a place of opportunity where there is ennoblement for all.

Individual Value

Work that is good for us is work that we actively look to be good for us. It may not be our perfect role, and if we're honest we are not perfect for any role as nobody is the finished article. But we can learn and grow in any role when we determine to let the challenges teach us rather than crush us. It's an attitude that sees the opportunities to learn and add value whether we are in our dream job or our fine-for-now job.

As an employee you gain far more from work than just a pay package. Long after your salary is spent, the value you continue to enjoy is in the training you received, the skills you've developed and the personal growth you made through the experiences that shaped you. We are whole people and what we learn and work and gain through training gets applied in every aspect of our lives and throughout our lives if we allow it to. What we do at work doesn't need to stay at work — unless of course it is secret or valuable data owned by the firm that we are forbidden from sharing!

Some of our training at work has direct applications, such as learning how to use software packages that then enable us to help produce things in a volunteer role or an admin task or family project. Sometimes our work develops us gradually and almost imperceptibly, like a plant that is watered and nurtured, but the life is visible and the growth over time is measurable.

I've watched both of my children develop in remarkable ways through the jobs they've had since leaving university. One of them had formal training while the other learnt on the job, but both have grown visibly in their confidence and competence as business professionals.

This investment in their personal development not only provides value in their professional careers – helping them perform well for their firms and stay in paid employment – but in their lives beyond the workplace. They've applied their training in lots of ways, such as starting an online magazine, leadership roles with charities, organising big events and even helping their dad build spreadsheets to analyse data!

Learning at work stays with us for life. I heard an example recently of a team which was under external examination. The director of the team never attempted to shift blame, but assured his team that it was his responsibility for decisions made and that he would take any consequences. As it happened, the examiners gave a clean bill of health, but the way that director acted stayed with the individual team member I spoke to, and will shape the way she acts when in a similar situation in the years to come.

> Who are you shaping for good?

We live in a culture that raises up some people higher than others. We talk about elevating a person to high office, either in a company as they join the C-Suite or a public body such as the judiciary or government. But for most of us there isn't going to be a letter from the Palace offering us a Knighthood or an appointment to the House

Individual Value

of Lords. I may not be called Sir Andrew, but am I being elevated in confidence and usefulness as a contributor to society?

There are a number of ways of developing as people and growing in stature through our work.

The Toolkit Test

Confidence at work is built by having clarity on the skills we have and the skills we need to develop. Like cars that need servicing and tuning so that they operate effectively, and like smartphones that need updates every now and then, our value in work is helped by tuning and updating skills.

There is a whole toolkit of opportunities to develop our skills. Our development at work may involve a formal programme that our employer provides, but it is also an attitude that we take in informal learning or in intentional reading, studying and practising of skills.

There are lots of opportunities available to listen to podcasts, read books or go to talks where we can build our expertise and hear insights. Meeting up with others to read and discuss a book is a great way of learning, and there are also plenty of courses and classes available that give opportunities to discover more and give more.

> What's in your skills development toolkit?

The Application Test

Those people who are growing as individuals at work are those who apply learnings every day. Whatever work we're in and whatever training opportunities are available to us, we can keep processing our daily work experiences and highlight the insights we gain from it. Becoming a continual learner is not just about gaining information, but then putting it into practice so that the data gained in our minds generates value in our lives.

Spend time at the end of each day thinking through what new information you've learnt, new insights you've gained, new experiences you've been challenged by or new skills you've developed. Then, once you've highlighted your new learning, think through how that will shape you going forward and how you can apply it in your work life and home life.

Using a journal to reflect can be a useful discipline and a way of pushing your thinking from what happened to what you learnt about yourself, others and the way things work well. That way your learning becomes wisdom and wisdom grows character that becomes part of you and continues adding value in daily life. Keep a record and review on a regular basis the progress you're making as a value generator.

Sometimes it's good to take a longer view and see how much we've grown. A process of continual assessment can be soul-destroying when all we track is tasks achieved. Reviewing and celebrating our individual growth can be soul-building. Rather than constantly

Individual Value

comparing ourselves to others and becoming competitive, it's life-giving to compare our own personal progress over time and become grateful.

> If you asked family and friends how you have developed through work, what would they say?

The Job Title Test
I love the way people have such creative job titles these days. My favourite examples include Head of First Impressions (for a receptionist) and Chief Servant (for a charity CEO). I'd like to be known as my organisation's CDO (Chief Dessert Officer), but unfortunately that doesn't comprehensively describe the value I'm generating day by day!

The point is that our job title should describe the point of our job and the meaningful value we're pouring our energies into. What does your job title communicate about the actual value of what you do? The phrase "the best spontaneity is rehearsed" is a good reminder that when people have a clear answer to a question, it indicates they've thought about it before more often than that they came up with a moment of brilliance with an off-the-cuff answer.

You may not be able to change your official job title but you can craft your reply when people ask you about your job. When people ask me what I do, I say something about opening people's eyes to see all the meaningful value their work generates and will often use a phrase such as "seeing a whole new world of value at work".

> How might you answer the question "what do you do?" in a more Whole Value way that describes the lasting value you generate?

STEP 2:
Refine with others

Personal transformation is inherently communal. Giving value to those around us and helping them grow helps us do the same. When I was younger, one of my hobbies was rock polishing. I'd collect interesting-looking rocks on our holiday treks and then pop them in my polishing machine. It worked by rotating a barrel full of rocks and some iron filings and water. The key was to have enough rocks in there so that they knocked against each other with each rotation of the barrel and smoothed each other.

Our personal growth is a similar process (except that we don't normally get locked in a rotating barrel). What we do find is that as we work with others and navigate difficult situations, our hard edges get removed and we help each other grow in wisdom as we learn together and from each other.

It's this two-way dynamic of receiving and giving value that makes work such an enriching experience. Most of us work with an employment contract that states not only what we will do, but

Individual Value

also what our employer will do for us. Work therefore isn't just a machine that squeezes outputs out of us, it's a collective of valuable people who develop value in each other.

President John F. Kennedy's inaugural address in 1961 included the memorable phrase to his fellow Americans: *"Ask not what your country can do for you – ask what you can do for your country"*. It's an inspiring idea and helps us be outward-looking in what we can do to contribute to others. However, there's an assumption built in that we already have the capacity to do things for our country and add value to the world. The challenge is to be resourced with value in order to provide value. Without assuming the right to correct JFK, perhaps we should ask what others can do for us so that we are equipped for what we can do for others.

Think back to your application process for your current job:

- Why did you apply and what were you looking for over and above a salary?
- Was the location important and why is that valuable to you?
- Was the working environment a factor and, again, how does the work culture affect your work experience?
- Was the training, development and opportunities to be stretched and progress important to your decision, and are your hopes being fulfilled?

As you go through those questions, I hope you are reminded of why you personally were attracted to the role and what you hoped to get out of the work as an individual. It's important to keep remembering that and keep reviewing what value we are taking away and being changed by.

It used to be the case that at a job interview the focus was entirely on proving what I can do for my prospective employer. The good news is that it hasn't stayed that way and now the tables are turned and people are asking what the employer can do for them. Are you asking that of your employer and how might you start that conversation in a productive and value-generating manner?

Of all the types of value we have the opportunity to generate, developing value in others is the most immediately applicable. When I talk to people and they say that they don't see much value in what they are doing, the "quick win" is to look at who they can be investing in. The value of our work is often in the conversations and encouragements that equip people to generate value for others.

If your work doesn't seem to be changing the world very much, remember that lives changed one conversation at a time grows lasting value.

Individual Value is something we can be adding to others when we see the value of others and the potential value in others. It's a shift of perspective as this example shows.

Individual Value

> Bob Chapman, a successful CEO of a multinational company, was sitting in the congregation of a wedding ceremony, watching a father walk his daughter down the aisle. He was thinking to himself how he knew exactly what that father was thinking as he approached the groom waiting to greet his bride.
>
> The father was thinking how much he loved his daughter and wanted the best for her and had equipped her to live a full life. Now he was expecting her husband to see, feel and act with the same love and concern for her thriving and wellbeing.
>
> Then the epiphany came as he realised that's the same for every member of his team – they are all somebody's precious child and he has the privilege and responsibility to care for them. Seeing the value of people as someone's precious child changed how he viewed people and the responsibilities of his CEO role.

How do you see your colleagues and those who report to you? I can't imagine you see yourself as a parent who gives a monthly allowance, helps them complete school assignments and picks them up from parties late at night, but taking a parental concern in other people's development is a lot more applicable to the workplace. Thinking of those you have responsibility towards, do you look to their interests and invest in their development?

The times I've grown at work have often been when people have invested in me not only by giving me responsibility, but also by giving me feedback on where I could have done things better. Both of these were gifts given to me by others who cared about me, encouraged me and took responsibility to develop me.

In the workplace we have opportunities to be developing each other and investing in others to create more Individual Value. Jane Adshead-Grant explains from her experience as an executive coach how we can take on this "parenting" role as encouraging, supporting and celebrating:

> *"If your son or daughter was not performing well at school, how would you be with them? Encourage them to think for themselves. Encourage them to come up with a solution for getting back on track. Encourage them to ask for support in practical skill building. Encourage them to develop a plan of action. Encourage them to hold themselves accountable.*
>
> *Support them to learn from when things didn't go well. Encourage them to develop themselves and consider where they could do better, more or differently to accomplish the results they want for themselves. Acknowledge and celebrate their successes along the way for their effort, achievements and accountability"*.[25]

The best tribute a child can give their parents is "my dad always advised me with wisdom, taught me with love and encouraged me to be the person I am today".

---

[25] Adshead-Grant, J. (2020, March 17). *Some leaders get it. Some don't. What can you do?* LinkedIn. https://www.linkedin.com/pulse/some-leaders-get-dont-what-can-you-do-jane-adshead-grant.

Individual Value

> Would you say the same if you replaced "my dad" with "my firm"? Would those you've managed or developed at work say the same if they replaced "my dad" with your name?

There are several ways of adding value to those individuals we work with and for.

The Inspiration Test

Who was your favourite educator when you were at school and why? Many people can think back to a teacher who made a difference in their lives and the most common reasons are that the teacher believed in them, inspired them and equipped them with tools for learning. This combination of feeling believed in, inspired and prepared to overcome any challenges are necessary for any learning to be effective.

Inspiration happens when you are shown the true value of what you are learning – both through the usefulness of its practical application and the beauty of the joy and wonder you experience. A great teacher is excited by what they are sharing and its potential to change the life of their students or mentees. This inspiration happens when, instead of being told "do what I say", you are shown exactly what they found so valuable about what they are giving you and invited you to consider how it can be valuable to you.

A good way to do this is to share our personal stories and experiences that explain what we found valuable, how it excited us, encouraged us and supported us through tough times. Talking with others about the insights we are gaining not only helps us clarify our learning, but also develops the insight as others add to it, and therefore we inspire confidence in each other as we explore and develop together.

> How are you inspiring confidence at work?

The Equipping Test
Properly investing in someone's development is about equipping them for life, not just one specific task or test. In school, which was better: the teachers who had you copy facts off the blackboard to memorise or the teachers who encouraged you to think how what you were learning could be useful in life or fit into the bigger picture? For me, it was the second group that truly changed my view on the world or my ability to take part in it.

A good teacher or mentor goes beyond the minimum requirement to teach you the "what" and "how" that you have to learn. They encourage you to think about and see the "why" – to identify the roots of the principles being taught and consider how they affect yourself, others and the world. When we teach fundamental principles, we give the value of wisdom which they can apply in whatever situation they face.

It's the difference between teaching principles of aerodynamics and teaching how to get cheap flight deals. The latter is a useful skill when the individual wants to book a seat on a plane, while the former gives them the knowledge needed to build a plane that will fly.

In every aspect of life there are principles and rules by which things operate – planes fly, deals are agreed, money is transferred, people are employed and so on. Equipping others with these principles enables them to fly whatever the circumstances.

> How are you equipping individuals with principles that will help them thrive?

The Mutual Empathy Test
During my undergraduate studies I completed a six-month work placement with a management consultancy firm. During my placement I was mentored by a partner called Angus Hislop. His care and investment was immensely valuable to me and my development.

I recently reflected with Angus on his mentoring of me[26] and he admitted it was more intuitive than organised. When he was a junior consultant, Angus had a similar relationship with a senior partner who invited him round for meals at his home. The value he experienced was infectious and was passed on to me – just as I am now passing on the benefits I experienced to you.

---

26 Andrew Baughen interview with Angus Hislop, 17 February 2021, London.

The key to a good mentoring relationship, according to Angus, is having a "mutual empathy" that gives a warmness to the relationship in contrast to people who were about the cold hard numbers and their career progression. A soulless view of people sees them as assets to sweat value out of. A soulful approach sees valuable individuals who we invest value in.

Angus believed in me – even though my skills on paper were laughably small at first. He trusted me with tasks and responsibilities with which I could learn and build my confidence. He put me on assignments as part of a team and gave me a role as researcher. I was also tasked with learning how to operate the firm's first Apple Mac, and my ability to get it to draw circles and boxes got me noticed by team members and clients alike!

This trust continued long past my placement as I was offered a job on completing my degree. When I started as a very junior full-time employee, Angus offered to be "my patron" and he did indeed take responsibility for encouraging me in my development over the years, advising me, training me and trusting me with more and more responsibility.

Being believed in ennobles you. When you feel that the person investing in you and teaching you both wants you to succeed and is confident you can, it gives you the self-confidence to try. Having someone clearly on your side, who believes in you and has the means to help you if needed, gives you the security to take risks and keep going when things might seem tough or even impossible.

Individual Value

Angus believed in me and therefore took time to relate to me as an individual and share his experience and wisdom. Our chats over a drink or a meal gave me a valuable insight into the person behind the suit and tie who was a husband and father, who had interests, hopes and dreams. He helped me see that life was more than work and that work is part of life.

> Who are you able to mentor and inspire? Who do you have a mutual empathy with?

STEP 3:
Seek lasting treasure

It's easy to miscalibrate our valuation of what's truly important and what is fleeting. How many times would I like to go back in time to my younger self and say: *"Andrew, stop obsessing about this, it's not that important"*. Hindsight is a wonderful thing, but there is a way to have foresight and that is by learning more about the true value worth us seeking as individuals and then experiencing the joy of lasting value.

In *The Chronicles of Narnia – The Voyage of the Dawn Treader*, C.S. Lewis introduces Lucy and Edmund's cousin, Eustace Scrubb. He is described as a quarrelsome, arrogant, greedy and jealous boy. When the Dawn Treader lands on one of the Lone Islands, Eustace wanders off to avoid helping with the work needed on the ship.

A Life's Work

He gets caught in a storm and hides in a dragon's cave, where he discovers piles of gold and jewels. He is captivated by the dragon's treasure and it arouses his greed. He fills his pockets, puts on a large golden bracelet and then goes to sleep on top of a pile of coins.

During his sleep, the desires of his inner self are manifest in his physical self and he becomes a dragon. He becomes shaped by his desires and his selfishness and greed are expressed in his new dragon form.

Eustace then wakes up to the horror of his predicament: he had sought to gain satisfaction of all his desires, but instead became captured by what he now saw was worthless treasure. He had taken a path that he thought would lead to happiness, but ended up on a path that led to misery. He had followed his heart and been told a lie.

He is only restored when Aslan, the great lion of Narnia, comes and tears away the dragon scales and gives him new clothes. He is given the opportunity to recalibrate his priorities and follow a path that will restore him as a human being with a full life to live.

While we are (probably) never going to find ourselves turned into a literal dragon, we might all find that the goals or value we have been chasing have got us stuck somewhere we never wanted to be. Imagine you go rock climbing and you get stuck on a cliff face. Your feet and hands are gripping the rock but you realise that you can't go any further up and it isn't safe to go back down either. At that moment you may feel safe on the solid rock, but it's an illusion.

Individual Value

A natural reaction might be to double-down and cling tighter to the rock. However, while rock may feel like a security, it's not going to save you. After all, it can't – it's just a rock. It won't lead you to the safety of firm ground or hold on to you to stop you falling. You're the one doing all the work holding on to it in fact – and all the energy that you are spending is keeping you stuck in the unpleasant situation.

The solution requires you to reassess whether what you're clinging on to and valuing is actually serving you. Imagine a helicopter then comes flying in and a man winches down, offering you his hand so he can pull you to safety. At that point you have a choice – keep gripping the rock or let go and hold on to the rescuer instead. You won't get to the safety of solid ground unless you give up your reliance on the rock's false security.

That's the problem with many things we seek in life and through our work. We all hold on to something and rely on it for meaning, value, significance and security. The question is whether or not it is worth holding on to and can really be relied upon. Is it a treasure of true value or a counterfeit?

The treasures we work to possess may be good and helpful to us at the time but aren't the ultimate solution that will meet our deepest needs. They may offer happiness in the moment but don't provide a security we can rely on or a meaning and significance that we can build our lives on.

These counterfeits may give a fleeting high of happiness, but one that quickly turns to a deep low, or they may provide a temporary security that gets pulled from under us. As Shakespeare puts it: *"All that glistens is not gold"*.

We find counterfeit treasures ultimately worthless for three reasons:

Problem 1: We expect counterfeits to deliver what they can't

Our hearts invest in treasures because we long for a deep sense of satisfaction and contentment. Many treasures are good things and do deliver to some extent. Family, friends, food, fitness and falling in love being some of them. These treasures add much to our lives and have great value.

But what if these things get disordered in priority so that we demand from them ultimate significance, security and satisfaction that they cannot deliver? This danger of "disordered loves" is when the real value of something is lost and an unrealistic value is expected. It's at the root of people singing "I can't get no satisfaction" and "I still haven't found what I'm looking for". Here are some examples:

- My job can turn from being an opportunity to practise my skills and do something useful into a competition to prove my worth and significance compared to others.
- Money can turn from being a means of exchange and a resource I steward to enable me and others to live into a means of buying

things that act as symbols of my status and success that project my significance even if I don't feel it inside.
- Other people can turn from being valuable individuals I seek to serve into servants at my disposal who can help me get what I want after which they are cut loose.

But it doesn't have to be this way. When we have a right view of the treasures in our life and how valuable they are, then we can invest in them by order of priority in a way that brings enjoyment and satisfaction rather than fear or pride. Our starting point with the treasures we have is to get our expectations right. What treasures are we investing in and why are we investing in them? What are we expecting from them and what are they expecting from us?

Problem 2: We try to control surface treasures instead of tackling deep desires

There's no point tackling flames if we don't get to the central cause that is fuelling the fire. In the same way, we can't tackle the things we serve if we don't get to the desires that compel our hearts to want those treasures so much. There are four deep desires: power, control, approval and comfort.

- **Power** is the desire to be of influence and looked to as successful. It can create an overdependence on personal significance and being "special". It causes anger fuelled by the fear of humiliation. In the workplace, it wants to win at all costs and can cause other people to feel used.

- **Control** is the desire for certainty and self-sufficiency. It can become an overemphasis on being able to do what is necessary through self-reliance. It causes anxiety fuelled by the fear of criticism. In the workplace, it wants to control the work environment and limit any factors that rely on other people who can end up feeling criticised and condemned.
- **Approval** is the desire for affirmation and acceptance. It can build an overdependence on the positive feedback of others. It causes avoidance of conflict and absorption of criticism fuelled by the fear of rejection. In the workplace, it doesn't tackle difficult issues and can build unhealthy reliance on some people or cause others to feel on the outside and not know what's really going on.
- **Comfort** is the desire for pleasure and immediate gratification. It can grow into an overemphasis on addictive behaviours. It causes avoidance of pain fuelled by a fear of stress. In the workplace, it can lead to avoiding taking responsibility and leaving other people feeling uncared for.

They are called deep desires because they are the reason behind the action – the inner motivating logic that shapes our attitudes and determines our choices of action. Each gives a different motivation for wanting things and each generates different hopes of gaining things or fears of losing these things. The problem comes when there's an overemphasis on one desire – an overdesire.

To take money as an example, we can value it because deep down we want to control our life or world and in that case we will save and

Individual Value

invest rather than spend. In contrast, we can value money because deep down we want access to social circles and so we spend on making ourselves more attractive to others. Alternatively, we can value money because it gives us the power and influence we desire deep down and we use it therefore as a power play. We can look down on people who use money in other ways than us, but actually are just as enslaved to it as them.

> Think about the treasure you are seeking and how that is shown in your work actions and purposes. What deep down desires are feeding your work – power, approval, comfort or control? What are the dangers of an overemphasis on one or more of these desires?

Problem 3: We end up feeding an addiction that will kill us
When having good becomes the ultimate goal we serve in itself, it drives us into the ground rather than us using it to grow. Like any addiction, the initial high of receiving the treasure fades, and not only that but we then need bigger and bigger hits to gain the same feelings. I know that from public speaking.

The high I get from the adrenaline of speaking at conferences or preaching at churches and then from the appreciation of people afterwards is a powerful high. But rather than enjoy it and keep myself grounded, the danger is that I start preparing talks in order to get a temporary buzz rather than to offer valuable thought and encouragement to others. Once I'm driven to obtain a treasure for selfish reasons that can never be satisfied I will be driven towards the destroyers of happiness at work – namely perfectionism, workaholism, indecision and controlling behaviours.[27]

If we want our work to produce lasting value then it's important to understand the difference between the good things that bring us enjoyment and the ultimate things that bring us life and feed our soul. Ultimately, the value of our work is in the treasures that last, such as love, joy and peace – it's in the value we gain as people growing in stature and contributing to society.

What would you say was the treasure of your heart? We often call loved ones "treasure" and we certainly invest lots of energy in children and family. But what about the treasures of our work life? What we invest in gaining in and through our work is the treasure our heart is set on possessing. It is the thing "*so central and essential to your life that, should you lose it, your life would hardly be worth living [and] has such a controlling position in your heart that you can spend most of your passion and energy, your emotional and financial resources, on it without a second thought*".[28]

One way to audit the treasure-seeking of our hearts is to ask what you focus on gaining and what you worry about losing. It's the things that spin in our mind and keep us awake that we are

---

27 See Keller, T. (2010) *Counterfeit Gods. When the empty promises of love, money and power let you down*. Hodder & Stoughton, London.

28 Keller, T. (2010) p.xviii.

Individual Value

concerned about with both mind and heart. It's those conversations and meetings when we feel ourselves getting animated with ideas or concerns and challenges to others that show what our heart cares about. It's the strong desire for something and a feeling of anger or sense of brokenness at its loss that shows the riches that we are looking for to satisfy our soul.

> What treasure can give you lasting joy?

There are several ways of seeking treasure that feeds the soul and gives us life.

The Imperative Test

The South African retail entrepreneur, Raymond Ackerman, describes how his first lecture as a commerce student opened with the words: *"Most of you are here to make money, but you won't. Not unless you have a moral mission"*.[29] His perspective on retail was shaped by an American retailer, Bernard Trujillo, who explained that at the time of the Great Depression, retailers were driven by the desire *"to alleviate the desperation of their fellow Americans. It was a moral imperative to drive down food prices because people were suffering"*.[30]

---

[29] Ackerman, R. (2010) *A sprat to catch a mackerel. Key principles to build your business.* Jonathan Ball Publishers, Jeppestown, SA. p.16.

[30] Ackerman, R. (2010) *A sprat to catch a mackerel. Key principles to build your business.* Jonathan Ball Publishers, Jeppestown, SA. p.17.

A Life's Work

A moral imperative is an action that we are compelled to do for reasons of virtue, character and ethics – we know it to be of crucial importance and can't stand by and do nothing as a result. Knowing the moral imperative of our work highlights the value we are commanded to pursue because it is the right thing to do and is generating lasting treasure.

> What is the moral imperative compelling your work? What treasure were you put on this planet to generate and what values shape the way you go about your purpose?

The Rest Test

Rest is a state of peace that goes beyond sleep or not working to a place of refreshing and even healing for the mind and soul. It is found in the deep security of being loved. It is built by having a thankfulness of heart as we see afresh the treasure in the everyday of what we do. It is enjoyed in rhythms of rest that start each day knowing that we're valued and end each day celebrating the beautiful gift of being of value to others.

One reason we can lack rest is that work can be hard. Sometimes we head into the eye of a storm and we ask ourselves the question: "Is it worth it?". We pour our energies into things but are our efforts worth it? When we're under pressure, knowing our work is worth it gives us an underlying peace and positive sense of purpose.

Individual Value

We also need that when things are going well. A restless heart is often caused by seeking something good but not then finding in practice what we're longing for. Instead of receiving the treasures worth giving our life to, we can end up with counterfeits which overpromise and underdeliver.

We need to choose wisely the treasures we want to invest in with all our heart so that we can focus our time on these life-giving activities. Peace of mind at the end of each day comes from looking back at the treasured time we spent doing what we love and generating value that was worth the effort.

> How do you slow down your racing mind and calm your restless heart? What valuable treasures give you security, contentment and peace deep in your soul?

A Life's Work

THE VALUE CONVERSATION: DAN
Passing on value

Growing and refining your Individual Value is not something you do alone. Supporting and mentoring others is a major part of the process as we saw in Step 2: Refine with others. However, sometimes it can be difficult to realise the value you're passing on to others. I was reminded of this recently through a conversation with Dan.

Dan works for a big firm as part of a delivery team for lots of clients. He'd heard me speak at an event and asked to meet me for lunch. As we talked it became clear that in his work he was going through the motions to ensure the work got done, clients were happy and his paycheck was guaranteed for another month.

He felt sure there must be more to work life than this but couldn't see further than being the best he could be at his daily routine. I started to ask him a bit about his week so far and he began to describe some of his workload. At one point, his whole manner changed and he became more alive as he described how he'd helped a junior member of the team who was struggling by taking time out to teach and encourage her.

He clearly loved the way that he had been able to have an impact on his colleague. It was also clear as I drilled down on the example how that wasn't in his job specification and wasn't something he could charge time for, but was something he gained value from and gave value through.

Dan went away from lunch with renewed vision for his work and the value he gives as a mentor of others. He'd seen through the portrait lens that focuses on faces and grasped the value of people developed as well as contracts signed.

Individual Value

I went away from lunch with a belly full of pizza and cheesecake. More importantly, however, Dan went away with a mind full of clarity about his role as a mentor and I went away with a heart full of delight at the value of mentoring others.

After the meeting, I found myself reflecting on mentorship; of my own mentors, such as Angus (who we met earlier), who had invested so much in me and my development. It made me realise how the way we're treated shapes how we treat others and how the Individual Value that we receive stays with us and continues to add value to others.

I also thought about a director called Nigel who had been my boss when I was a young management consultant. Nigel used to check my work and comment in the margins of documents I'd written. He would correct my spelling and then most often just write two words at various points which have stayed with me ever since. The two words were "so what?"

I can't tell you how often I think about those two words or how often I've told the story of Nigel's challenge to others. As a result of being challenged to consider "so what", I learnt how to push my thinking further. Rather than just stating the obvious, I learnt to dig deeper and seek the implications. Instead of just adding information, enable its application.

The delight to me is that the Individual Value given to me by Nigel continues to shape the way I work and hopefully the value of this book to you and the value you will continue to give as you answer the "so what" challenge.

Relational Value

Chapter Seven

Relational Value

Strengthening collaboration, practising generous values, connecting with other stakeholders.
Growing a culture of thriving, promoting mental health, aligning with personal values.

We have looked through the telephoto lens at the value of what we do both in being useful and beautiful. We have also looked at work through the portrait lens that brings people into view. In the previous section we focused on the Individual Value we can each develop. Now we are going to look at the other aspect of the portrait lens – the Relational Value we generate as we connect with and work alongside others in our workplaces.

> Two are better than one, because they have a good return for their labour: if either of them falls down, one can help the other up. But pity anyone who falls and has no one to help them up.
>
> Though one may be overpowered, two can defend themselves. A cord of three strands is not quickly broken.
>
> **Ecclesiastes 4:9–10, 12**

Two is better than one. To be a human being means to live within a relational ecosystem where we rely on others as well as being relied on by others, and we receive from others as well as giving to others. But we can still all too easily slip into living independent lives where the rights of the individual are championed over the collective good.

Have you ever had that feeling of being surrounded by people and yet very alone – lost in a crowd without connection to anyone? I had that feeling on one trip to New York to see friends who announced just before I arrived that they had to leave town for something (I tried not to take it personally!). As a result, I had a week in the city that never sleeps and is full of people everywhere without talking to anyone. I became so starved of relationship that when a greeter at a store asked me how I was doing I stopped to chat as if they were a long-lost friend!

Being alone surrounded by people is very different from being alone in isolation. The added ingredient I realised as I walked around the Big Apple is that people pass by you because in that moment I had no value to them. If I'd been one of their friends or family, there would be lots of value in stopping to catch up. If I'd been a celebrity, I might have got many requests to stop for a selfie. For me, however, short of handing out free doughnuts, there was no reason for people to take any interest in yet another Englishman in New York.

The reason it's painful is because we need to know we are of value and the way we know that is by being shown value by others. I know I'm of value as a human being in theory but am more alive when I experience value in relationship. Work is a primary setting in which we experience and express value in relationship with others. As we work we cooperate with others and are therefore more alive as a thinking, feeling and relating human being.

Being human and cooperation are inextricably linked. The portrait lens looks at Individual and Relational Value – we need both aspects. We grow as individuals but also need to be aware that individualism disconnects us from the relationships through which we thrive.

It's an interesting tendency we have to want to break free and declare our unilateral independence from others, when the route to happiness is healthy dependence. But it doesn't have to be that way and we weren't born that way. While we start life dependent on others and end life dependent on others, between those two points we often try to live as if we were independent of others!

As Professor John Wyatt puts it:

> *"You and I came into the world as helpless beings, utterly dependent on the love and care of people we did not choose. We go through a phase in our lives when other people depend on us. We protect them, care for them, feed them, pay for them. And then most of us will end our physical lives utterly dependent on the love and care of others. We will need other people to feed us, protect us and care for us. This is not terrible,*

degrading, inhuman reality; it is part of the design. It is part of the narrative of a human life".[31]

People vary in how much they get their energy from social interaction or need alone time. Some individuals need more personal space than others. But a defining characteristic of human beings from the start is that we are social creatures who depend on others. Research has shown that "having positive relationships is one of the most important factors shaping people's personal wellbeing".[32] We are who we are truly made to be when we operate in an interdependent community.

Human beings flourish in connected relationships and prolonged isolation can be very harmful. Isolation may not involve being put in a cell on your own for weeks on end, but it can feel like that when the people you work with don't connect with you or seek to relate with you. It's not as much about the physical closeness of other humans, it's about the emotional connection with others.

Multiple research studies have shown that "well-connected people live longer, and enjoy more productive lives than those who are socially isolated".[33] A greater sense of belonging and

---

31 Wyatt, J. (2018) *Dying well.* Inter-varsity Press, London. p.70.

32 Measuring national well-being in the UK: international comparisons, 2019. Office for National Statistics, 6 March 2019.

33 Research by the Relationships Foundation. Quoted in *r thinking*. (n.d.). Relationships Foundation. accessed 8 March 2020, from https://relationshipsfoundation.org/r-thinking/.

Relational Value

social engagement leads to increased happiness, self-esteem and motivation. On the other hand, being on the outside and unnoticed at work makes us feel like an irrelevant object that others don't care about, rather than a person who belongs and is wanted.

This is a sensitive subject because we may feel overwhelmed by the number of people we work with or underconfident about approaching others and starting a conversation. We may feel they are too busy or that we'll be wasting their time. But connecting with others we work with is a valuable use of time. Building relationships has three powerful benefits:

- *Relationships humanise*
  As people interact they see the human beings behind the technical problems and the actual users behind the data points. Relationships give people a sense of being noticed, listened to and cared about. Being understood and understanding others is core to being human and the myriad of interactions we have with the power to build each other up or destroy. We all know that feeling when someone takes the energy out of the room. But what about you? Are you contributing ideas and energy to the room?

- *Relationships clarify*
  It's as we listen to each other and understand different perspectives that we become more equipped to deliver products and solutions which are shaped around a diversity of need. As we work with people with disabilities we are more understanding

of what it's like to overcome challenges. As we encounter the hurt of people facing discrimination we are more energised to eradicate the harmful attitudes and practices embedded within our organisation and society.

- *Relationships unify*
  An unwillingness in the workplace to share information and collaborate breeds competitiveness and gaming behaviours which can lead to resentment and feelings of isolation. In contrast, a people-centric culture sees opportunities to help and serve others on the team as a joy and privilege. Strong relationships in organisations allow cooperation and the combining of knowledge, talents and strengths that achieve more together than is possible apart.

At its core, work is a cooperative endeavour. Even if we do our particular work tasks in isolation, we rarely produce something without needing resources, systems or functions provided by others. The question is whether we're working with others in a relationally healthy way that adds value to the whole.

> What would you say are the benefits you gain and give from working with others? How are you being a positive influence on the relational culture of your workplace?

We may feel that the organisation we work for is so vast and the culture is so set that we can't change anything. But when we focus on our immediate circle of influence then the opportunities become clearer. Just like a member of parliament has a constituency they represent or a pastor has a parish they serve, so we have a relational sphere in which we operate.

How we operate in that sphere matters. As we explored earlier when looking at the pie baking priority, there are four views of value that shape how we work: guarding, grabbing, giving away or generating value. The way we turn up to work impacts others we work with and the ways we encourage, assist, train and challenge others applies our belief in the value of relationships and the Relational Value we generate in practice.

Wellbeing is linked to how we relate to people which is rooted in how we see people. Applying the four views of value clarifies four relational postures we can take at work:

- *The individualist posture* has very little interest in the needs of others and sees people as assets to gain from or absorbers of time and energy to keep away from. It avoids relationships unless there is personal gain and values time alone to get on with their agenda.
- *The competitive posture* is suspicious of people, sees others as a threat and wants to beat them in whatever they are racing to gain. It is constantly comparing with others and aiming to have more than them of whatever is most valued.
- *The saviour posture* sees others at work with compassion and wants to meet their needs and solve their problems. It doesn't

look to personal gain except the value of being the one at the centre.
- *The generative posture* sees others at work as colleagues and looks to gain the most value from cooperative working where it is all for one and one for all. It sees the value of relationships with others and considers cooperative work to be the most natural expression of human endeavour.

Which posture we take has a marked effect on the value we add to others and the value we gain from working with others and therefore on our wellbeing.

It may seem efficient to go into work early before anyone else is there in order to get my work done – lots of work can get done that way. But the only work that is being measured here is personal task completion. I can't do any work that requires face-to-face contact. Nor can I do any work that involves ideas and feedback from others. What seems efficient is actually mechanical rather than human-shaped. It might hit targets, but it doesn't feed the soul.

It's common for inspirational leaders of entrepreneurial companies to talk about loving their latest innovation. But what about loving the people they work with? Is your workplace a location you go to get tasks done or a relational hub where you enjoy creating value with others?

> Would you say that your place of work is beautiful on the inside?

Steps to Relational Value

As with Individual Value explored earlier, there is a hierarchy we can use to study the value we have the opportunity of generating by working with others and building a culture of value. Toxic cultures and individualistic behaviours destroy value for the whole, even if more is gained for self. We all have an opportunity therefore to contribute to Relational Value in our workplace by the way we work with others.

The starting level is building generative cultures and cooperative working relationships.

We are relational beings but relationships don't just happen, they need building, deepening and restoring. The starting point therefore is to relate to others as co-workers who are invested together in a common goal and build teams that function well together.

At the middle level, we relate well when the values of our hearts are engaged – rather than just the jobs we need other people's help with. Taking teams from functional to connected requires care and is about building on foundations that are infused with strong values of honesty, openness and trust.

At its deepest level, relationships that thrive are ones with a level of closeness and trust that goes well beyond team-building techniques. Deep relationships practise grace which doesn't hold mistakes against people but offers forgiveness and a willingness to rebuild when things go wrong.

Let's look at each of these three levels in turn and explore the steps to developing Relational Value at work.

STEP 1:
Make teamwork

Healthy teamwork isn't a nice-to-have added ingredient, it's a vital element of an organisation's success. Research shows that trust is linked to innovation as people share ideas and take risks together. It is also found that high-trust workplaces "find it much easier to embrace organisational change – they can adapt faster and will achieve better levels of employee engagement".[34]

Deep levels of transparency and trust encourage people to collaborate freely, share willingly and listen effectively. Where relationships are poor and distant then a lack of trust can lead to individuals holding back from sharing valuable information or listening to others with suspicion, competitiveness or even resentment.

---

[34] Hope-Hailey, V. (2012, March). *Where has all the trust gone?* CIPD. https://www.cipd.org/globalassets/media/knowledge/knowledge-hub/reports/where-has-all-the-trust-gone_2012-sop_tcm18-9644.pdf Foreword, p.3.

Relational Value

Our early experiences of teamwork and leadership models have a deep influence over our practice of acting in a team. Understanding these influences is vital if we are going to add value in our workplaces as we interact with others in teams.

Once upon a time there were three people who worked together in a team...

Alan was in a meeting with work colleagues who were disagreeing with him. He felt frustration welling up in him and wanted to shout that his idea was the best and why didn't they just listen and accept it. Throughout his career Alan had tried to avoid conflict but found himself causing it because he was unable to understand why people couldn't see that what he was doing was for the best.

This pattern got worse and worse until colleagues left, which Alan thought was for the best as he set about recruiting new team members who he was confident would agree with his approach. At first, new staff, such as Kyle, agreed with Alan's inspirational and innovative ideas.

But as time went on they got increasingly disheartened with the Alan-centric model and, rather than confront Alan, Kyle complained to other team members and left quietly as soon as a new job opportunity arose. But toxic gossip didn't do the team any favours and Alan was never confronted. Until now.

The disagreement at this meeting was different as battle-lines were drawn by Zach, a relatively new member of the team. He wasn't going to accept Alan's view and had heard what colleagues thought about their boss and he seized on an opportunity to tame the beast.

One way to unravel this scenario is to look at the models of teamwork that our characters had learnt from. For Alan, his earliest model of team was his family, where he enjoyed the leeway of being the youngest and got away with all sorts of things unchallenged, such as being allowed to win at board games even when he knew he didn't deserve to. As a result, Alan has the confidence to lead, but never learned to accept alternative perspectives.

For Kyle, his earliest model was Scout camp where he learnt to follow instructions and lead by example. Over the years he had experienced teams led by inspirational leaders who people followed willingly and trusted fully. He accepted that Alan may not have had their level of character or ability, but recognised some great ideas which he wanted to support and be involved in. Kyle is a supportive team player, but never learnt that challenging authority is sometimes important.

Zach had come from a military family and was used to obeying orders and dealing with problems decisively, even if the costs and casualties were high. He had also spent time in social work and was very attuned to destructive behaviours. He saw the hidden conflict and wanted to battle it out rather than allow it to fester any longer.

Relational Value

Zach has the social intelligence and perspective to recognise the problem and the perspective to fix things but took an approach which is too confrontational and public.

But understanding is only the beginning. We don't normally have the power to change the teams we're in and even going to the extent that Kyle did of switching jobs doesn't necessarily answer the issues which are in all probability going to resurface elsewhere as long as people are people.

What we do have the power to do is to change the way we act within teams. We can learn, as Alan needed, to listen to other perspectives and value the opinion of each member. We can grow, as Kyle needed, in confidence to express opinions and challenge unhelpful team behaviours. We can develop, as Zach needed, our skills in promoting new healthy team dynamics and behaviours.

As one individual amongst many, we may not feel able to influence the culture of our organisation but teams provide a smaller and more relational context for adding value to others and being a positive influence. It's often the place where we come alive as we rely on others and they rely on us.

Teamworking makes our heart sing and expresses what it means to be human as we trust others to achieve a shared aim and switch from "me" language to "we" thinking. It's the delight of seeing a great sports team play where they are passing to each other, supporting each other and working together towards a common goal. And it's when a goal is scored that the whole team rightly celebrates.

> How are you contributing as a team player and what delight does it bring you and others?

There are several ways of building teams with Relational Value.

The Connectedness Test

Erica Dhawan has developed the idea of "connectional intelligence": the power to create value, meaning and results by combining the insights, skills and resources of our people. We live connected lives with constant access to a range of digital platforms. Connection is a way of life and sharing with others is a daily habit.

> *Millennials don't just embody an age of difference – they embody a whole new connected mindset that's here to stay.*
>
> ERICA DHAWAN[35]

The connected mindset looks to the collective for information and solutions, rather than a particular individual or even an expert institution. You find that when chatting with a group of friends and a question is raised. It's discussed for a while, but then someone does a quick search on their phone and provides more answers. By pulling in perspectives not just from your friend group, but the wider internet as well, a clearer picture is formed.

---

35 *The Drucker Forum Special Report 2017.* LID Publishing, London. p.12.

Connective intelligence in the workplace is about drawing in the ideas of a diverse range of people and perspectives into our work because we value them and their insights. It's about leveraging current networks and creating new connections with a willingness to share in a two-way exchange of ideas and resources. The challenge is to ensure the connection we have with people is genuine, trusting and caring.

Just having people in a network is of little value if there's no relationship with them. Therefore, when looking at our connectedness, it is useful to assess the quality of the relationships we have within each network. But how can something so subjective as the quality of a relationship be defined?

The Relationships Foundation suggests five aspects that determine the quality of relationships:

- **Communication:** the level of direct contact and communicating there is between people.
- **Continuity:** the regularity of dialogue between people.
- **Knowledge:** the personal connection and how well the people actually and honestly know each other.
- **Power:** whether power is abused within the relationship such as how much information is withheld and used against others.

- ***Purpose:*** the extent to which people in the relationship are working together with common values.[36]

It may not be that every one of your relationships rate 5/5 across the board – and that's OK! However, these relational aspects can be used to do an assessment of the quality of relationships you have within your workplace and highlight areas for development. If you realise that you need to work on a relationship, by discovering the aspects which could be stronger, you can discover the best place in which to start.

> What networks of relationships are you connected to and how are they an opportunity to give and receive value?

The Tea Break Test
Harry's first job as an architect was with a local authority. They gave him a project of looking at a piece of public land which was seen as dangerous and underused, and asked him to come up with rejuvenation ideas. Harry was the young upstart and found himself at a desk surrounded by people he considered hardened by time and cynical about progress. He was dismissive of them and felt they didn't respect his ideas as he hadn't "done the time".

---

[36] Talk by Jonathan Rushworth on 'Transforming Capitalism from Within' at KPMG London Offices, December 2013.

Relational Value

But then he made a surprising discovery. He started joining in with tea breaks and chatting to his colleagues. He got to know them as people rather than just work colleagues and they started opening up to Harry. Harry realised that they joined the department with ideas of change and progress just the same as he had. He realised that their vision and experience was invaluable to him.

After endless cups of tea and a fair few conversations in the smoking corner, they started giving Harry ideas on his project from their experience. Most crucially, Harry was willing to listen and shape his ideas from the combined wisdom in the room which had the depth to be approved and create valuable change.

Organisations are full of people who have lots of new ideas and in the right circumstances are willing to share a vulnerability and openness to the unexpected.

> What is the context in your workplace where people will open up and share their experience and insights? What is the team break?

The Joy Test

One of the great joys of work is helping others to thrive. A joyful illustration for me is Glen, who joined my team fresh off the plane from Australia. He was like a wild horse – full of incredible talent that needed harnessing. At first I tried to control and train by telling him what he was doing wrong. But our relationship suffered as a result and I soon realised that it was better to resource him, give him opportunities and to encourage him in some of his outlandish ideas.

It's as I look back that I see some of the fruits of our time working together. For example, I created a lot of short films as part of my work and trained Glen to help not only as an assistant but also to direct and produce films himself. Another example is a risk I took when I asked Glen to speak at one of our big Christmas carols events. He recently tweeted about the valuable lessons he gained from doing that talk and learning from the mixed response of people to his overly combative approach.

Glen now runs an amazing organisation that produces brilliant short films with a big audience. As I watch his success, my joy is that I added value to him in his formative years, both by training and also by trusting him to learn on the job. The joy is in seeing how the small amount of value I added has multiplied and continues to multiply.

> Are you gaining in value and experiencing joy as you add value to others?

Relational Value

STEP 2:
Build relationships on values

When building any structure, getting the foundations right is crucial to its success. Foundations may be invisible and buried underground but their influence on the integrity of the building is very evident – especially in a storm. I have friends who live in a tall apartment building that sways in the wind. I'm sure they've never seen the foundations, but I also know they are glad they can rely on them.

Just as buildings have foundations, so do organisations. These are often written down in the founding documents and in recent times founding principles are written on a wall. What makes mottos foundational to an organisation is when they are applied and practised. In the same way that the foundations of a building give structural integrity to the building, these mottos and values give integrity to the way we work, why we do what we do, how we treat each other and where we're going.

When foundation principles are practised, they act like a computer operating system. A computer operating system manages the software and hardware, allows access to the processing centre and memory stores, and provides an interface for users to perform tasks.

In the same way, every workplace has an operating system that shapes:

- the assumptions, beliefs and values held;
- the decisions made, actions taken and processes managed;
- the ways people interact and their effectiveness at getting tasks done.

The question is whether the operating system is based on strong and wise foundations that will give a structural integrity to the way the organisation acts and develops – and more personally, the way we act and develop within the organisation. For better or worse, the way organisations operate – with clarity or chaos – has a direct impact on us.

The problem comes when our beliefs and attitudes are at odds with how the company we work for operates – when our values system and its operating system collide. Jeffrey Pfeffer, a professor at Stanford, argues that our wellbeing is shaped by how the organisations we work for choose to organise themselves.

Just as the United Nations agreed to a Declaration of Human Rights, the people we work with are human beings with human rights. As Professor Pfeffer puts it:

> "These fundamental human rights and moral precepts do not disappear when one becomes an employee. We have, therefore,

a moral obligation to work to ensure that our places of employment build rather than break down the human spirit".[37]

Relational culture at work matters. It can lead to thriving or can destroy us. I have a friend who went to work as an accountant for a fast-growing business and was initially thrilled by the fun atmosphere in the office and the motivated work colleagues. But gradually she became deeply unhappy. She found that the information she needed to do her job was never forthcoming and rather than her being able to clarify numbers, they remained obscure. It left her feeling not trusted, excluded from conversations and that she was a risk to be managed rather than a colleague to be valued.

In the end she left and a few months later the firm was declared bankrupt due to a massive fraud. That explained why numbers were not clear and why she was kept away from what was really going on. Being treated without trust or value is dehumanising.

The management guru Peter Drucker emphasised that an organisation isn't managing things, but people, and that leading is a liberal art requiring an understanding of the human condition. Each

---

37 Pfeffer, J. (2010). *Business and the spirit: Management practices that sustain values*, in Giacalone, R.A. and Jurkiewicz, C.L. (eds), *The handbook of workplace spirituality and organizational performance*, New York: M.E. Sharpe, p.40 https://jeffreypfeffer.com/wp-content/uploads/2019/10/Business-Spirit-27.pdf.

of us has a responsibility for the wellbeing of others and therefore need to understand their physical, emotional and relational needs.

A healthy workplace has humanity running through what is made, as well as how we treat each other. It recognises that we are emotional and spiritual as well as functional beings.

The tragedy is that relational culture can get ignored, especially when growth is fast and the pressing needs are plenty.

We can say: "yes, I know we're not treating each other well but we're fully focused on scaling right now. It can wait until things are quieter". However, culture can't wait, and even if the quieter day comes (which is unlikely), the culture you start with can get hardwired into the organisation. If you don't work on building a healthy relational culture, it can become toxic.

Wellbeing is a shared responsibility. We can all work on improving health and resilience at work. Some of the greatest achievements in our work are found in how we've helped others thrive.

> What ways are you promoting wellbeing in your workplace?

The Gallup Organisation has gathered extensive information on what brings wellbeing in the workplace. Their conclusion is that 68 per cent of employees are struggling or suffering from mental health challenges at work. Symptoms include experience during a lot of the previous day of worry (41 per cent), stress (43 per cent),

Relational Value

anger (24 per cent) and sadness (23 per cent).[38] One of the elements that makes up overall wellbeing is liking what you do each day and Gallup suggests that employers play a key role in developing strengths, encouraging friendship and social interaction, providing education, promoting physical activity and celebrating community service. As Jim Cliffton, the CEO of Gallup, puts it:

> "*Your manager has more impact on your health han your doctor*".[39]

There are several ways we can be a positive influence on relational culture and work with values that promote wellbeing.

The Seat Test

One of the easiest ways to add value in your workplace and build wellbeing for others is to say to a colleague "take a seat". Approaching conversations with an open mind and having the emotional intelligence to realise when someone is being supportive and gracious was a lesson I learnt early in my career.

My first work experience role was in the accounts department of a US oil company. I remember needing to get some information on a

---

38 Gallup (2021). *State of the global workplace 2021 Report*. Available at https://bendchamber.org/wp-content/uploads/2021/12/state-of-the-global-workplace-2021-download.pdf.

39 Quoted in Gallup webinar "*Wellbeing in a post-pandemic world: How leaders can improve employee wellbeing and engagement.*" March 16, 2021.

number in a spreadsheet and I booked a meeting with the head of the department concerned. At the appointed time I went up to the executive floor where his office was situated and knocked on the door. I heard him say "enter" and I found myself in a swanky office with a massive desk in the middle and two comfy chairs facing the desk. The director told me to take a seat.

But I then made my crass error. I said straight back, "*oh it would be much easier if I showed you the number on the sheet*" as I marched round his desk, stood next to him, thrust the document in his face and pointed at the figure in question. He politely told me the answer, I thanked him equally politely and left the room.

But that wasn't the end of it! Before I'd even got back to my office, my boss had received a phone call from the director explaining what had just happened. My boss then sat me down, no questioning this time, and explained to me that the director had wanted me to sit so that he could get to know me and give me some of his time and experience.

I'd completely misunderstood the intention behind the instruction to sit and had missed out on an invitation to receive relational capital of getting to know a director and gaining from his wisdom – capital he was willing to invest in me and would have produced an ongoing return in me. But rather than receive that I just received an answer to a question. I missed out on the value available.

Relational Value

But the beauty of the story is that the director didn't let go of the opportunity to give. He could have thought, "what a fool" and been glad I didn't waste any more of his time. But instead he took time to follow up so I'd learn. He chose to forgive my mistake and work to help me learn from it rather than be defined by it. Why was that? Because he had a concern for my wellbeing. He saw the whole me rather than just an analyst in search of some data.

That act of kindness has stayed with me in tens of thousands of meetings I have had subsequently – all because the director said "take a seat" and when I didn't, he bothered to pick up the phone.

We can add immense value by taking time with a co-worker and find out how they are doing in body, mind and soul. We make "seat time" a regular practice in our working day when we sit down with someone and chat. This might simply involve saying "take a seat" or it might be going for a meal or drink and getting out of the immediate work environment or it might be going further afield and spending quality time with someone by enjoying a walk together. Rather than say "take a hike" to someone at work, why not say "let's go on a hike"!

The Transparency Test
Safe relationships are ones where we can be honest, real and unburden emotionally. Finding people who understand you and are interested in your good as a person rather than a function is priceless treasure.

We all play different parts and often have a number of work roles – the question is whether those public performances are the genuine us or a mask we've put on. Sometimes it's difficult to know ourselves, and often the parts we play in work and outside work get mingled together, especially with home working becoming more common.

The challenge therefore is to know where the separation lies between personal and professional lives, and have relationships at work based on trust and vulnerability where you can unmask and be yourself.

Building honest relationships in teams includes a willingness to think critically, ask questions and be reflective. As Alvesson and Spicer put it in their book *The Stupidity Paradox*:

> *"This means querying the assumptions that we make, asking for and being prepared to give justifications, and considering the outcomes and broader meaning of what we do. Doing this requires mature thinking – something that is sorely lacking in most of our organisations as well as society at large".*[40]

Honest relationships enable honest feedback. Being willing to ask what is actually going on avoids "groupthink" and roots out destructive behaviours and relational issues that are affecting the team. Research shows that effective feedback contains the

---

40 Alvesson, M. and Spicer, A. (2016) *The stupidity paradox*. Profile Books, London. p.224.

willingness to speak truth with compassion and a genuine concern for the person's development. This in turn breeds trust and openness in the future and a willingness to seek help.

Transparency and honesty is about pointing out the bad but also the good. There is power in giving and in receiving praise. Praise builds people up by appreciating aspects of who they are and what they've done. It shows you are noticed and highlights the valuable contribution you are making. Is praise a regular practice in your workplace? How often do you notice someone who has done a good job and thank them?

Research by McKinsey management consultants concludes that: *"Best practices indicate managers should have ongoing development discussions with their employees at least monthly, or even more frequently. But the value of these discussions only happens if they are development focused and actionable"*.[41]

We give great value to others by creating an environment where people can be honest and look for help knowing it will be responded to with kindness and positive action.

---

41 Chowdhury, S., Hancock, B. and Williams, O. (February 1, 2021) *Unlocking the true value of effective feedback conversations* https://www.mckinsey.com/business-functions/organization/our-insights/the-organization-blog/unlocking-the-true-value-of-effective-feed-back-conversations. Accessed 9 February 2021.

> How can you contribute to work relationships in ways that build trust and transparency at their core? Are there safe work relationships where you can be honest, real and unburden emotionally?

The Village Test

Rich Ward is an expert in building healthy work cultures and has applied the idea that it takes a village to raise a child with the phrase "*It takes generations to make a workplace*".[42] The workplace is a context in which to develop as a person, especially within a network of people across the generations and from very different social backgrounds. The benefit of working where not everyone is "people like us" is the village mentality of social cohesion with the global mentality of different perspectives.

We spend a considerable proportion of our waking hours at work and the work we do presents us with opportunities to interact with different people who think differently from us. Our workplaces therefore have a valuable role in forming our view of the world, ourselves and others as we experience a diversity of views and are given the space to consider them and learn how to be more inclusive.

Character isn't static in people but develops as we navigate challenges, and our values are formed as we reflect on how we will

---

[42] Andrew Baughen interview with Richard Ward, Director of RAW Unlimited. London 9 November 2020.

navigate challenges in the future. Working with others can provide a safe context in which our values are challenged and our attitudes are shaped. We learn from each other and our character is refined by each other.

> How are you benefiting from this village mentality at work and the diversity of views that you experience?

STEP 3:
Infuse relationships with grace

Healthy work environments are places of reconciliation, where broken relationships are mended. There are many ways that relationships can become broken – even in great corporate cultures people act with selfishness or unintentionally do things that cause relational harm. But the good news is that we can all play a role in restoring healthy relationships at work.

Often relational breakdown can be fixed by resolving the issue causing the conflict. But sometimes it's not possible to fix quickly or to fix at all. In those cases, another aspect of restoring relationships comes into play – showing the kindness of grace. Grace is about covering the person at fault with forgiveness and giving a fresh start.

In the movie *The Dark Knight Rises* Catwoman, Selina Kyle, wants to get hold of the Clean Slate Program, which will erase her criminal past, allowing her to move on. That's what grace does. Grace accepts that the mistake has happened and learns from it, but then puts it in the past and accepts that any guilt and fault has been dealt with so people can move on without blame hanging over them in the future.

As a child I remember disobeying my dad and rather than saying sorry, deciding to run away. As I was only 6 I didn't go very far, but set up home in a shed next to the house. After what seemed like hours, but was probably minutes, I started to feel hungry and having heard both parents calling my name from further and further away I realised I wasn't going to be found in my hiding place.

So I set off on the long journey home and went to find my dad. I said "sorry" and will never forget the experience of what happened next. My dad scooped me up in his arms, gave me a big hug and said "I love you". That experience of grace and restored relationship stayed with me and was repeated many times over many years. It was a gift I received and then began to willingly offer to others, especially when I became the father in the relationship.

When our children were younger we practised what we called grace breaks. It was something any member of the family could ask for when something bad had been done and everyone was getting cross and blaming others. Once the request for a grace break was made and accepted we would all spin round on the spot to rewind to before the situation had started and reset the day from there with the messy part removed and never mentioned again.

Sometimes when the children asked for a grace break I didn't feel like giving them one as I wanted them to be told off still, but that's what grace is – unmerited favour. And what does grace do? Build healthy and strong relationships of openness, trust and love. Forgiveness brings healing and grace restores life. Now that's value worth generating!

There are several ways of working with grace.

The Mistake Test
There is nothing like the gift of forgiveness – it brings relational healing because it means the mistake or wrong action is in the past and there is freedom to live without the consequences hanging over us. Sometimes mistakes can't be forgiven and the consequences have to be faced but we still have the option of showing kindness to people which recognises the truth of the situation but still wants to bring restoration to the person.

It starts with a willingness to admit and a confidence of what will happen when we do that. Sorry may be the hardest word but it shouldn't be as it's the most powerful word when the reply is forgiveness. Countless people and countless workplaces miss out on receiving that freedom of mistakes forgiven because of an unwillingness to admit mistakes, an unwillingness to forgive mistakes or an unwillingness to learn and grow from mistakes.

A career-ending mistake can happen with the smallest of errors when it gets magnified and weaponised. A CEO of a major UK bank found that out in the convivial setting of a charity dinner. She responded to a news report about why her bank had cancelled the account of a well-known political figure. As it turned out the answer she gave was not the complete picture and the person asking the question was a journalist who had the means to distribute the story far and fast. What followed was a string of newspaper headlines and even questions asked in the UK parliament. Bank statements, corrections and claims ended with her removal as CEO and as adviser on several government working groups.

The truth is that she made an error of judgement. The truth is also that she was leading the bank through a very positive review of purpose and values. And to apply to us, the truth is that we've all done things far worse – and so had all those calling for her to be sacked.

> When we see mistakes, is our response to condemn or forgive?

Toto Wolff, Team Director of the Mercedes Formula 1 team in 2019, said of their success:

> *"It's about putting everything together and not leaving one stone unturned, having a no-blame culture, empowering [people], even when it's difficult sometimes when you would rather control things. I think the strengths go very deep, values that*

Relational Value

are ingrained in the teams that you can't put on a PowerPoint and say 'now we are empowered'".[43]

No blame doesn't mean no care about mistakes. It means not wasting energy on condemning people that could be spent on solving the problem. As Toto Wolff says, the way we handle problems comes out of deeply ingrained values.

The values ingrained within our workplaces are shown in the way mistakes are dealt with. Is there blame which leads to fear of owning up, hiding of mistakes and an unwillingness to learn for the future? Or is the value of learning rather than condemning seen and gained?

It is sometimes easier, especially if you're a manager, to step in when a mistake is made by someone and fix it yourself. But the real value is gained by teaching and helping someone to fix it so that they learn and also feel they've contributed to putting things right.

How we respond to mistakes, particularly ones which cause loss or put us under pressure, is deeply connected to how we see people. If people are seen as units of production then people who make mistakes are seen as faulty units that are either fixed or replaced. But if people are seen as valuable human beings then mistakes are

---

[43] Barretto, L. (14 October 2019) *The culture behind Mercedes' greatness* https://www.formula1.com/en/latest/article.the-culture-behind-mercedes-greatness.6VW1gfx5hsjRZUC731T77x.html.

seen as an opportunity to learn, develop and strengthen them and others around them.

> How have you been shown grace at work and how did it change you? How are you contributing to a working environment which cares about people and shows grace?

The Generosity Test
> *Each of our stakeholders is essential. We commit to deliver value to all of them, for the future success of our companies, our communities and our country.*

The Business Roundtable Statement on the Purpose of a Corporation, 2019[44]

You can tell a lot about the state of an organisation's heart and soul by how it treats people who supply it with basic goods and services. Is our attitude to suppliers transactional or thoroughly relational?

Transactional motivation keeps the cost to a minimum and only pays when the invoice deadline looms. The people in the transaction are invisible and supplies are scanned in at the delivery door with only the mildest of human contact. Relational motivation acknowledges

---

[44] https://opportunity.businessroundtable.org/wp-content/uploads/2020/06/BRT-Statement-on-the-Purpose-of-a-Corporation-with-Signatures.pdf.

the people supplying us and cares about them. Conversation is of benefit to both parties.

I'm not suggesting we spend hours chit-chatting away about last night's TV and exchanging pictures of our cats. That would most often destroy value and create wasteful inefficiency. But there is value in knowing your suppliers so that the service they give and benefit you both receive from the relationship is maximised – it doesn't cost anything to remember and use someone's name, for example.

The cooperative business ecosystem starts with a spirit of generosity. In his book *7 Habits of Highly Effective People*, Steve Covey talks about an "abundance mentality" which believes there is "plenty for everyone". Abundance is an attitude to work and business that comes from a heart of generosity and often stands counter to the prevailing "dog eat dog" culture.

Jodi Glickman wrote in the Harvard Business Review[45] that "Generous people share information readily, share credit often, and give of their time and expertise easily". She finds that a spirit of generosity comes from a consistent and high-level work ethic often based on an understanding of higher calling. She also suggests that

---

45 Glickman, J. (2011, June 8). *Be generous at work*. Harvard Business Review. Retrieved February 13, 2024, from https://hbr.org/2011/06/be-generous-at-work.html.

generosity is based on effective communication that readily shares information and collaboration.

As a result, generosity of spirit builds trust and enables better-informed decisions to be made. It leads to a win-win situation in a business context: both the person in question and those around them stand to gain from it.

> How do your work practices have a sensitivity towards the needs of others and a willing generosity in meeting those needs with value?

Relational Value

THE VALUE CONVERSATION: LAUREN[46]
Value in Ventura

During my research, I have visited many different organisations and have experienced many different first impressions. For some interviews, I've been kept waiting in a waiting room with a minimalist business chic vibe while they try to find the person who had agreed to meet me. In other offices I am greeted by a barrage of security measures with photos taken, NDAs signed and escorts provided to watch my every move.

Some offices have huge gleaming signs with their name on at the roadside entrance, others have a wall in the entrance lobby covered in photos of smiling staff members. Some offer coffee, others a sweet from a jar and still others nothing at all.

What is certain is that first impressions tell a story of culture and values. Which is why the greeting I received when I met Lauren at Patagonia was so distinctive and illustrative.

First off, the office was in a very ordinary street in the middle of Ventura, right next door to the original shop and workshop where the production of garments began. The workshop is still there and is used on occasion, and the setting has remained the same – the beach is still down the road and the mountains for hikes and other adventures are also still up the street. The message is clear that the firm has stayed close to its roots, both physically and culturally.

My second impression was provided by the meet-and-greet. I got a text to say that I should let the person I was meeting know when I arrived, and she would meet me on the street. As it happened, before

---

46 Andrew Baughen interview with Lauren Thompson, 14 March 2022.

A Life's Work

I even had time to send a reply, Lauren was crossing the street with arm outstretched laughing as she told me she recognised me from watching my TEDx talk earlier that morning.

What did all this teach me? Patagonia treats people personally – giving out mobile numbers, learning something about me in preparation and not expecting me to find my way through security channels. Now, you might say that what I've described could never happen in a big corporate and I'm being naïve. But Patagonia's revenues are $1 billion so it's not exactly a mom and pop shop!

Patagonia generates plenty of financial value but does that with a team of people who are also generating and enjoying plenty of Relational Value. The firm has managed to keep a family culture thanks to the way staff interact without the business side becoming in any way amateur. Two contributors to family culture that I heard about were the influence of founders on site and the presence of children, also on site.

Lauren described how the regular messages from founder Malinda Chouinard, affectionately known as *Malindagrams*, are *"very beloved because we can tell how deeply she cares about us beyond what we produce at the company. They are messages of how to care for ourselves, connect to nature, and even parenting advice such as managing kids' screen time"*. She also described having the boss' kids in the same class as her children and how *"it's hard to be mad when you see colleagues caring for your family"*. It's a helpful insight that doing things together outside of work mode and showing practical care and compassion to each other in other settings builds a friendship that is like family rather than just functional.

Relational Value

Recent staff engagement surveys on "reasons for being here" give three clear answers: products, people and mission. Value is added in abundance when the ethos of the products and the ethos of the organisation are closely aligned and resonate with those who work on the products for the organisation. If the mission of the organisation is to enable people to enjoy the planet in all sorts of activities and to care for the planet in use of resources, then staff will be engaged when they are passionate about these things as well.

One contributor to employee engagement is the encouragement to feed in ideas such as the "don't buy this jacket" campaign and the Black Friday offer where all sales went to the mission of the firm and $11 million was given away. A famous example was when a wholesale manager decided not to offer goods with another company's branding on anymore because it was felt that people such as entrepreneurs walking around Silicon Valley streets in Patagonia active sports lines with a corporate logo on weren't in line with their mission.

The fact that this decision went viral is perhaps not as surprising as the fact that the manager made the decision without reference to senior leadership. Lots of red tape wasn't necessary since the vision and purpose is shared and permission to make decisions is given.

What is the lesson we can learn and apply?

That Relational Value develops when vision inspires culture and culture shapes action. For example, the staff know that the founders "genuinely care about the environment for their grandkids" and therefore adopt the same principles in the ways they work, such as being resistant to jumping into trends and offering a free garment repair service.

A Life's Work

That vision of garments having a lifetime of use is reflected in practice in the way staff tend to wear clothes to work that have seen many adventures. As Lauren said: *"a patch is like a badge of honour with a story attached of getting it when climbing El Capitan or whatever"*. The culture set by the firm's vision is embedded into the staff's attitudes and actions. Their passion was clear in everyone I met who didn't just wear Patagonia clothes as a dutiful uniform but as an inhabited lifestyle.

Communal Value

Chapter Eight

Communal Value

> *Repairing what is broken, renewing systems, removing injustice, improving outcomes.*
> *Impacting communities, widening inclusion, developing society and shaping wise choices.*

It's now time to take the third lens out of our camera bag. The telephoto lens showed us the value of what we do and highlighted the aspects of usefulness and beauty. The portrait lens highlighted the value work brings to us and the value we bring to work, both as individuals and in relationship with others.

The third lens offers a wide angle and takes in all the value our work has in wider society both now (Communal Value) and in the future (Generational Value). We're going to start with the present and look at the broad impact of what we do as individuals and as part of the organisations we work for.

> *One noticeable outgrowth of humanity's spiritual qualities is the development of culture and the ongoing advancement of*

technology and civilization. While many animal species use tools, form communities, and even divide certain roles and responsibilities with the community, the community life that developed among humans represents a whole new level of complexity, diversity, and growth. Human culture bursts upon the scene.[47]

Anthropologists describe cultural "big bang" events that followed the arrival of humans on Earth. Early examples include a huge leap in tool technology, the starting of clothing and jewellery production, and the first appearance of sophisticated art, music and religious practices. These culture-forming events fuelled a movement of people looking to the good of others as they went from hunter-gathering to farming and from subsistence farming to cooperative agriculture. The more the primaeval people grew in number, the greater need there was to work together and the move started from homestead to cities.

Establishing cities enabled safety through mutual care and stability through organisation. The ancient city was defined by a wall. Those inside the wall were protected from enemies and external threats. Within the wall the development and organisation of civic society brought together a wide range of inhabitants contributing to the wellbeing of the city – whether in education, arts, justice, commerce or health.

---

47 Ross, H. (2014) *Navigating Genesis, a scientist's journey through Genesis 1–11.* Reasons To Believe Press, Covina, CA. p.72.

Communal Value

The history of mankind is an amazing story of progress as civilisations developed, but our story also tells of empires that became agents of terrible oppression and destruction. We have the power to pursue both construction and destruction, reconciliation and separation, restoring and rejecting.

That is true for us as individuals as well as for us collectively as people working together as an organisation. The soulful approach is about being conscious of our responsibility for the wellbeing of society. This goes beyond social responsibility as a department and instead takes an integrated view of business as part of society – a two-way relationship of reliance where one flourishes as the other gives and vice versa.

In my research, I have often found a link between the wider impact of an organisation and its founding narrative. Organisations established with a focus on generating Communal Value bake an aspiration to be of value into the founding principles so that it becomes their heartbeat.

The founding narrative acts as "a grand story" that is retold continually as new people join the firm and is part of the brand that people experience as they do business with the firm. It grounds an organisation's strategic direction, internal culture, approach to serving customers and attitude to other stakeholders.

Investigating the founding narrative of the organisations we work for helps us understand why some things, actions and contributions are so valued. The more we understand the founding narrative, the more value we find in our work. We see how our work is part of that grand story and the grand story part of our story of value. Contributing to a grand story widens our vision, from a specific activity we are working on to the transforming impact on society, and therefore Communal Value that our work has.

> *Every society has a 'cultural economy', a set of public sectors in which ideas and practices are forged that direct how people live in the culture. These include the academy, business, the arts, the media, law and government.*[48]

A society is a large group of people who share norms and values that connect them as they live together interdependently and work together for the common good. The spheres of influence within a society include local and national government, businesses large and small, trade unions, universities and schools, local and national charities, and many others. Then there is the media and increasingly the tech companies that gather data, distribute information and connect people together.

Understanding the different spheres of influence within which we work and operate helps us see the impacts we are having within each sphere and have an intentional and valuable influence for

---

48 Keller, T. (2020) *How to reach the West again.* Redeemer City to City, New York. p.48.

good. One of the issues that stops us seeing our influence is that the impact isn't necessarily immediately obvious.

Impact can be direct, such as an arrow hitting a target, or can be a ripple effect that grows over time, such as a pebble hitting the water and making wider and wider ripples. Some work does have an immediate impact on society, such as developing products that improve health or nutrition. But for many of us, our work has a less direct impact but is still making a valuable contribution to society, such as providing telecoms services or education.

One of my great joys is meeting people who tell me how they heard me talk or read something I wrote and how that helped them in their work and impacted their life. It reminds me that we often don't know the impact we have, for good or ill.

> What ripples of value is your work making in the wider world and in your different spheres of influence?

One question worth asking is whether business has a role in impacting society or whether it should keep out of the way and just make money. William Blake's "Jerusalem" became the anthem of the suffragette movement and is now often sung at national events from sports matches to royal weddings. It was written as a prologue to a poem about a new society in England's green and pleasant land that stands in contrast to the "dark, Satanic mills" of the Industrial Revolution. But that portrayal of business as bad and the enemy of society is not the full story. One rich set of examples that combines monetary and community value is found in the history of the Quaker businesses.

In the great Quaker firms, business magnates had a real vision for the relationship of business, family, workforce, locality and wider society.[49]

The Quakers remind us that there is a spiritual heart to business life which can transform society. They were motivated by a distinctive moral code of honesty and integrity. This directly affected the way they conducted business – not least with a commitment to fixed prices and an aversion to debt. In addition, they cared for those that worked for them, pioneers of pension schemes, sick pay and decent working conditions.

The brick and mortar outworking of this was seen in the building of model villages by such as the Quaker Cadbury brothers, George and Richard, who moved their chocolate factory from the centre of Birmingham to Bournville, where they also built houses, schools, baths and libraries to "ameliorate the conditions of the labouring classes".[50]

---

[49] Turnbull, R.D. (2014). *Quaker capitalism: Lessons for today.* Oxford: Centre for Enterprise, Markets and Ethics.

[50] Turnbull (2014) p.41. Quoting Henslowe, P. (1984) *Ninety years on: An account of the Bournville Village Trust*, Birmingham: Bournville Village Trust.

The Cadbury brothers and other enlightened entrepreneurs, Quaker or otherwise, had a big picture of life. They deployed their moral conscience in the conduct of business and a belief that their business activities contributed to a flourishing society. They viewed business as a calling and sought to improve society through a life of faith and service.

In today's society it is unlikely there is a social need for communal bath houses anymore, but the challenge of translating our desire for the common good of society into practical action that has a tangible impact remains.

Steps to Communal Value

As with the other types of value we've explored, there is a hierarchy we can use to study the impact we have the opportunity of generating in the community and wider society for the common good.

At the starting level, our wider impact is in the ways our work makes practical contributions to the culture and structures of society. Growing this wider impact starts with understanding the needs of the context in which we operate and then deciding how best we can contribute.

At the middle level, we look under the surface at some of the issues people face and the barriers to growth and thriving of people. We see how we can have an impact by repairing what is broken, renewing systems and values or restoring the structures of society.

At its deepest level, our work is of most impact when we care personally about the issues we see in the world around us and become engaged personally in making a difference. This level can be costly as it means giving of ourselves to others, but the benefit in seeing transformation in others is joy to the soul.

Let's look at each of these three levels in turn and explore the steps to work with Communal Value that has impact in communities.

STEP 1:
Shape culture

Culture is one of those words that means different things to different people. It can be used as another word for the arts, in scientific circles it is the actions we take to maintain an environment for growth, as in "culture cells". But more accurately, culture is a description of a particular way of life of a particular group of people.

The key is that every group of people has a culture – it's not that some are "cultured" and the rest are "uncultured". Describing opera and ballet as "high culture" unhelpfully paints others as "lowbrow". We're all cultured by the way of life we follow.

Our culture is the way we behave, what we believe and how we organise ourselves. Our work therefore is informed by and forms culture. We don't make culture but we shape it by the structures we build and we influence it by the stories we tell. As Andy Crouch, a writer and investor in cultural renewal, puts it:

Communal Value

"Culture is what we make of the world. Culture is, first of all, the name for our relentless, restless human effort to take the world as it's given to us and make something else".[51]

We all have opportunities to shape the culture in which people live, work and have their being. Sometimes we shape culture directly through our work in education, government or the arts that improves the quality and effectiveness of structures, policies and practices. In other roles we have a less direct but equally important impact on culture. The ways our products are used, the ways our customers live, the ways our supply chains connect with people and the ways we empower people to make good choices are all examples of how our work cultivates culture. To use a gardening analogy, some of us plant, some water, some weed, some add nutrients, but all are involved in cultivating life.

One barrier to us being cultivators of culture is when we condemn it or try to cut ourselves off from it. Andy Crouch uses the example of a movie theatre with eight screens, all showing films a particular cultural group disagrees with because each attacks their particular beliefs. He suggests that instead of petitioning for the movies to be banned or staying away and not adding to the viewing figures,

---

51 Crouch, A. (2008) *Culture makers. Recovering our creative calling*. Inter Varsity Press, Downers Grove, Illinois. p.23.

the positive approach is to make new movies that do express your values and influence the moviegoer's beliefs for the better.[52]

Building culture starts with a belief in society and the part we can play. It then takes responsibility for developing the structures of education, sanitation, security and government that enable society to flourish. Being a cultivator is a mindset switch from heaping on criticism to being part of the solution.

Do you believe you can be a force for good in society? It's the difference between working on an advert that sells a product and working on one that tells a story of how life together can be. Teaching people how to read may not seem as high profile a job as sending a person into space, but by improving skills you are propelling them so they can reach for the stars!

There's been a major emphasis recently on impact businesses with a social purpose. That often means that social impact is prioritised over financial gain or that the financial gain is measured by how many rough sleepers are taken off the streets or how many people leaving prison reoffend.

But while there is a role for social enterprises, social good shouldn't be their exclusive responsibility. From the beginning of their formation, organisations have been collectives of culture makers

---

52 http://andy-crouch.com/articles/being_culture_makers Accessed 19 January 2024.

and shapers. Business operates with what is called a "social licence from society" which means that there is a two-way agreement that business serves society and society benefits from business, but also that business employs people from local communities and relies on customers from local communities.

C. William Pollard, author of *The Soul of The Firm*, describes how we have responsibility in our work for "crafting a culture of character and recognising that the business firm has a duty of care not only to the customers it serves but also to the societies within which it operates".[53]

> What opportunities do you have to model a culture of character?

The challenging idea is that we're not just selling people products but also shaping people's lives. It's challenging because it reminds us that our work has consequences in terms of the way people relate. Building a strong and just society is a responsibility we share. We can't just say, "I operate the social media site, if they use it to criticise and disrespect others that isn't my problem", because it is!

Having a societal purpose is nothing new. For example, Panasonic refers to a "basic management objective", back in 1929:

---

53 Pollard, C.W. (2014) *The tides of life. Learning to lead and serve as you navigate the currents of life.* Crossway, Weaton, Illinois. p.101.

"*While giving careful consideration to harmony between profit and social justice, we aim to devote ourselves to the development of national industry, to foster progress and to promote the general welfare of society*".[54]

More recently, Panasonic has set its philosophy in these terms:

"*Recognizing our responsibilities as industrialists, we will devote ourselves to the progress and development of society and the well-being of people through our business activities, thereby enhancing the quality of life throughout the world*".[55]

One of my passions is helping people see that they can be of impact right here and right now. That whatever situation they are in, whichever company they work for and whatever job they do day to day (assuming it's not fundamentally harmful), they can be shaping culture and having an impact in wider society. Would you agree with that? How are you a culture cultivator day by day?

There are several ways of being a cultivator of culture and adding value to society.

---

54 https://www.panasonic.com/global/corporate/history/chronicle/1929.html.

55 https://www.panasonic.com/global/corporate/history/chronicle/1929.html.

Communal Value

The Influencer Test

There is a whole new category of job that has been formed in recent times that has the title "influencer". I would argue that there have always been influencers and that we are all influences in some shape or form. But that said, the ability to influence a large number of people has never been easier and the skill of being a positive influencer has never been more important.

In the movie *Man of Steel*, Superman's father, Jor'El, is explaining his son's mission to Earth as giving an example to follow so that the people of Earth will join him in the light. Showing people an example of a better world and presenting a pathway to that reality is one of the privileges we get to enjoy at work.

The people who have been of most influence on me are those who demonstrate a better way of acting in a situation and what attitudes such as kindness look like in practice. I've learnt that it's in the small things, such as being patient when clients are being impossible, that trust is built and long-term influence is achieved. I've learnt that putting in the time and effort to really understand an issue and all the dynamics creates work that engages hearts and shapes lives. I've also learnt that bothering to explain why as well as what equips people to be culture cultivators as well.

Showing people an example to follow starts by knowing the better ways of working and understanding the reason certain practices lead to distinct outcomes. We don't want to just tell people to do what we do without a reason or an appreciation of how to make decisions along the way.

It's the difference between demonstrating how to draw a picture of a mouse which people copy stroke by stroke, and showing people the principles so they can draw whatever they choose in the future. We need to know the principles in order to embed wisdom and healthy practices in the wider world we serve.

A helpful way of seeing and celebrating the lasting value of our work is to review the influence your work is having on cultural norms, attitudes and behaviours. Not just influencing people to buy things, but do things, not just consume but create, not just to repeat what they've been told, but contribute ideas. That way our great work is multiplying the ability of others to do great things.

Knowing who we are influencing is key, as is knowing how we want to influence and where we are heading. Here are some influencer questions to think through:

- Who are we aiming to influence and why?
- What healthy practices are we aiming to encourage?
- What wisdom do we want to be forming?
- What new ways of thinking, relating and living can we show?
- What is the gap between the current reality and the ideal?
- What are the barriers to change?
- How could we be an agent of change?

Communal Value

We do not want to be seen as moral police but our mandate is to act in ways that enhance people's lives by connecting them to information, people, practical tools and other resources that shape values and build values.

> How are you enabling culture making? How are you influencing the decisions people make so they are able to act with wisdom and make a positive difference?

The Inclusion Test

In our culture it's easy for people to be assessed and ranked according to the wealth and power they hold, with the top people featured in rankings and the very pinnacle making it on to the cover of a magazine. What is harder is for the voice of the marginalised to be heard. When our desire is to generate value we will want to share value with others and include more people in the process of value generation.

Where is your heart for the excluded? It may depend on how much we have experienced exclusion ourselves. One of the stressful moments for a school child is the picking of sports teams. At my school, the two captains took turns to pick players. On many occasions it got down to the ones they'd prefer not to pick – which usually included me, unless extreme height was a specific qualifying factor.

Exclusion is stressful when others are preferred over you. But on the other hand, there's something very wonderful about including people even when they are not the most qualified. Inclusive growth looks to ensure that every part of society and the economy benefit from growth.

It's about nobody being left behind and thinking with principles of fairness that prioritises the needs of those with less power or voice. Inclusive growth sees all people as being valuable and deserving of opportunity. It takes responsibility to include those who are harder to reach – particularly those excluded for social, financial and political reasons.

> How can you include more people in the value your work produces? Are there unreached groups about which you need to think creatively in order to include them in the benefits your organisation already offers others?

The Social End Test
Part of the new way of thinking about business is actually a return to the old way of seeing business – reintroducing the idea of social conscience as an inherent part of an organisation's thinking, rather than a box-ticking exercise to satisfy some Corporate Social Responsibility (CSR) requirements.

Management guru Peter Drucker describes a corporation which has "co-ordinated human efforts to a social end" where "everybody

Communal Value

from the boss to the sweeper must be seen as equally necessary to the success of the common enterprise".[56] The idea of coordinated human effort underlines how social purpose is the responsibility of everyone rather than just the few or a particular department.

That involves the whole firm knowing their social purpose and reflecting that in its mission or vision statements and strategic priorities. It requires effort to make social gains to the lives of people in society, especially when shareholders are only interested in their financial gains. The more people within an organisation bang the desk and say "this is what we do because this is who we are", the more that wider value will be part of the end gains rather than a means to a single end of financial gain.

> What is the social end of the organisation you work for? What vital role does your work make in building wider social value?

STEP 2:
Repair and restore

I love TV shows that repair and restore a property or someone's dearly loved items, such as a piece of furniture that has been in the family for generations. The highlight is the big reveal. It's

---

[56] Maciariello, J.A. and Linkletter, K.E. (2011) *Drucker's lost art of management. Peter Drucker's timeless vision for building effective organizations.* McGraw-Hill, New York. p.30.

fascinating to see how the owners react when they see their renewed items and their joy in the value that has been created. Rarely do the owners then sell the item they took for repair. Their benefit is in the restoration.

We have seen so far that we can make an impact in society and change the game by innovating new value. We can also have impact and increase value through restoration of broken or lost value, the mending process. It's about taking something lacking in useful purpose and restoring its value. How you restore value will depend on why the value became lost in the first place. Restoration therefore looks to the value of what could be and has a joy in seeing things come back to life, whether that be a classic car back on the track or a redundant worker who has been retrained and reinvigorated.

Restoration can get forgotten in a disposable culture where things that are broken are discarded in favour of something new. Gone are the days of going to the repair shop for many items or even when an engineer comes to fix a problem with an appliance or car. The solution is often to replace a part rather than attempt a more specific fix.

There are many reasons for this trend. For example, the progress of technology means that equipment is often out of date compared to the newer models, as well as the complexity of solid state systems which can't be easily repaired outside a highly sophisticated workshop.

Communal Value

But the logic behind why we dispose rather than renew doesn't sit easily with our values as people. We don't like being discarded ourselves, nor do we appreciate something we have invested in and lived with being placed on a scrapheap. Our human longing is to resolve issues with people rather than just dump them, and repair brokenness rather than let the loss continue. Part of our calling as people is to restore value where it has been lost.

The emphasis of restoration is on returning to value. If an expert restores an old painting, he removes the dirt, repairs cracks, replaces missing paint and revives the magnificent colours. If an engineer restores a computer, she removes unnecessary data, repairs corrupted software, replaces missing applications and revives the speed of processing. In both cases, restoring brings the item back to the maker's original intention and gives the user a full experience as intended. This is true of objects and is even more transformational when people are restored. Repairing the structures of society empowers people to take a full part in society.

Restoring value repairs missing value but also releases from anything that is preventing value – an activity often known as redemption. Redemption replaces bad attributes with good, suffering with happiness, captivity with freedom. It releases a person, people or organisation from a debt that is holding them back and preventing them from being of value. So you redeem a prisoner by paying their fine on their behalf or you redeem the deposit you've prepaid on a drinks bottle or rental car by returning to the owner. We have the opportunity to empower people by releasing them from the power systems, cultural assumptions and harmful practices that are holding them back.

I had a personal experience of being involved in a redemptive project that released people from debt and gave financial freedom when I was a student studying business finance. I did some work experience with a development agency and ended up being sent to Pakistan for a few months. I'd studied basic accounting modules but to my horror was asked when I arrived to set up a whole accounting system for a brick company. I don't suppose the basic ledgers I created lasted very long before being upgraded to something more efficient, but the experience lasted with me for a lifetime. It wasn't the work itself that I remember, but what value the work was enabling.

The brick company I did some work for was pioneering a way of releasing people from what today would be called modern-day slavery – a term unheard of then because the reality of bonded labour was still normalised in some circles. The company made bricks but its purpose was to change lives. The founders realised that there were many people working for traditional brick kilns to repay a debt that had often been passed from generation to generation with no hope of ever being repaid. Whole families of workers were bonded to the brick kiln and were trapped by excessive lending practices they had fallen victim to.

Today, this practice of using unpayable debts to effectively enslave people is illegal under modern slavery laws. But at the time, the

Communal Value

investors I worked for saw the need to resolve an injustice and created a solution of paying back the debt and then once people were free they were offered employment that valued them and their brick-making skills, treated them well and paid a fair and living wage. I saw first hand and at the start of my career the redemptive potential of business.

Redemption believes in people and believes that people can be redeemed. It looks to release people from situations that put limits on their future and empower them to have control over their lives and make decisions about their future with confidence.

Sometimes that vision for redemption is front and centre, such as with the chain of coffee shops in London called Redemption Roasters. It was set up as a roastery in a prison to train offenders in coffee-industry skills with the aim of reducing reoffending in the UK. They follow a four-stage Redemption Model[57]:

- Employ up to five prison residents at a time and teach them practical skills in coffee roasting, production and logistics. These skills build their confidence and improve their self-esteem. The pay is above the standard rate and a portion is set aside to access upon release from prison, giving a headstart when reintegrating into society.
- Run barista academies in prisons, teaching residents all the skills they need to become coffee masters. Students are awarded

---

57 www.redemptionroasters.com/our-mission/ accessed 10 February 2024.

a grade and given one-to-one help transitioning into sustainable employment.
- Run barista academies in the community, giving skills to prevent risk of offending and offering participants the best start as baristas.
- Place prison leavers in a suitable role, either in one of their coffee shops or within their network of partners. Provide wellbeing, developmental, financial and legal support.

In your workplace, redemption may be front and centre or it may be more of a belief that is integrated into every activity of the business. However redemption is positioned, the question we can explore is whether we believe in redemption and are willing to take the risk on people in order to see the rewards in people who are given a new start.

Profits made may be a measure of financial performance but lives changed is a great measure of impact. In your work are you looking to maximise financial income as well as redemption impact?

A redemption mindset isn't satisfied with leaving things undone and just making do. When it encounters a mess, injustice, division or anger, it doesn't offer criticism or leave it to someone else to fix. Instead, it acts to resolve things – offering justice, reconciliation and mercy. Working with a redemption mindset looks beyond an immediate decision to the consequences of our work actions.

Communal Value

Part of our thriving as workers is to know that the organisations we work for and with share a redemption mindset. Business as usual keeps within the law, business with a redemption perspective looks beyond the minimum requirements of the law and actively removes injustice.

In some models of business, caring for those on the margins of society or caring about harmful issues and structures would not be seen as not the organisation's concern. In a generative model of business, desiring redemption is seen as the organisation's heartbeat.

> How important is redemption to you personally and how much is that the concern of the organisation where you work?

There are several ways of working with a redemptive mindset that seeks to repair and restore.

The Kintsugi Test
The restoration process may involve repairing damage and mending broken parts exactly as the original, but often restoration introduces new materials or technology which makes the item as good as new but different from the original or even better than new.

Kintsugi is the Japanese art of mending broken ceramics with a lacquer resin which highlights the repair in gold or another colour and gives the restored item a particular beauty as a result. There is a particular beauty in restoration which demonstrates how much we value something by making the often costly commitments of time, energy and sacrifice to put back together and restore lost value.

> What value are you willing to invest your work efforts and time in restoring? Why is it important to you? What is the golden thread that enhances the value you've restored?

The Popeye Test

There is someone near and dear to me who has said many times after visiting friends' houses: "I couldn't live in all that mess". It's not a phrase of malice towards them but an observation that some of us are wired to see and solve mess, and others of us live with and tolerate mess. The tidiness of your house is one thing, and mostly a matter of personal opinion, but the mess and harm in our world is a more universal issue.

Popeye is a character from a cartoon I used to watch when I was a boy. Popeye got angry when he saw injustice and said "that will not do", but then acted by eating a can of spinach – out popped his muscles and he was ready to act. When you see problems do you have a Popeye moment of saying "that will not do" and getting involved by being the solution?

It's easy to get overwhelmed by all the problems in the world and wonder how we can make a difference. It's also hard to choose between all the causes competing for our time, money and attention.

Communal Value

One answer is to make a choice and invest in a cause you have a personal connection with and are in a position to help with.

The following steps help you to identify your project:

1. Think through what issues you are passionate about and what injustice drives you to see resolved.
2. Discuss with others the issues people face that make you call out "that will not do" and you have the resources to resolve; the enslaving practices you could free people from; the dehumanising practices that you or your organisation could rethink and embed a culture of care where everybody matters.
3. Choose something that is broken and that you have the skills and capacity to help fix.
4. Prioritise helping people facing issues that are harming their wellbeing and holding them back from thriving.
5. Make restoration a regular part of your innovation thinking and priorities.

The Take Home Test

The saying goes that charity begins at home. That may be true in many cases, but charity also starts at work and then is applied at home, as Rowan (who we met at the start of the book) points out.

> "When I graduated, I knew some theories and had a passion to help the world run better but didn't know how to or have the confidence to add value and effect change. In my work I have learned a range of technical, relational and commercial skills

through both formal training and on-the-job experience which mean I now feel much more confident in my ability to help people and companies identify problems and make positive changes in response to them.

These skills and experiences have also helped me in my personal life. It has given me confidence in relationships, personal financial management and the roles I feel comfortable to take in my groups out of work. For example, I have been much more confident to take on leadership roles and start my own initiatives out of work linked to my passion for helping people solve problems".[58]

As we saw earlier when exploring Individual Value, the skills of repairing and restoring value that we develop at work are transferable and applicable in different spheres of life. So, for example:

- Listening skills build up marriages and families.
- Arbitration and restorative skills lead to lasting relationships.
- Leadership and finance skills equip people to add value in community programmes.
- Creativity and planning skills bring vibrancy to local community initiatives.

---

58 Andrew Baughen interview with Rowan Smith, London 30 May 2020.

Communal Value

Adding value in the whole of life adds significance to our work as we see how it connects to our personal lives, family lives and professional lives.

Sometimes the skills learnt at work can be directly applied to projects when, for example, people involved in finance at work can offer financial advice as a volunteer at a local debt counselling service.

Sometimes skills learnt at work can be indirectly applied, for example using strategy and leadership skills in helping a local charity or being a school governor or on the board of a not-for-profit organisation. Oftentimes, however, the application is more inherent in people's ability to live with a redemptive mindset in all their roles and responsibilities at home and in the community.

> What skills have you developed at work that can be applied outside of the workplace?

STEP 3:
See, care, act

From the outset, the engine driving this book is an idea that became a passion which has been honed into a message that can inspire action. An idea on its own is nice to have but lacks impact. It would be extremely ironic if this book about discovering work with meaningful value had no impact on you and how you see the immense value of your work – or led to you having no more impact on others than you had before.

How do we stop that from happening? By ensuring that the ideas we think about spark a fire of passion in us that compels us to action. Returning to our *Popeye Test* from Step 2 of this section, saying "*that will not do*" is a statement of the heart as well as logic. We're not just analysing the technical characteristics of a problem, we're feeling with a passion the consequences and difficulties caused as long as the situation does continue.

One common factor in the people I've interviewed, who have had great impact in solving societal problems and bringing transformation to many people, is that they started out with a disturbance playing on their mind that got lodged in their heart and became the passion of their work.

James is a lawyer who has had a significant impact in tackling the scourge of modern-day slavery. I first met him when he had newly arrived in London to start a job with a city law firm. My abiding memory is of a man full of energy, madly in love with his girlfriend and full of ambition to live a good life and make his mark on the world.

Fast forward 25 years and our paths crossed again. I noticed James was giving a lecture about modern-day slavery and thought I'd go along. What delighted me was seeing the same James, now a little older and married to the love of his life, with ambitions that had a clearer focus. He was fuelled by a passion for justice that went beyond the day-to-day work of a lawyer. James spoke with urgency about how people were facing the injustice of slavery in our cities – not just a long time ago and in a land far away. He was harnessing his energies and investing his time in something really important to him.

However, he hadn't started out even thinking or caring about the issue. He explained how the epiphany moment that this issue was one he could personally do something about only came when he was 33 years old. While recovering from treatment for a recurrence of non-Hodgkin lymphoma he attended an anti-slavery presentation and found himself far more open to the issue than he had been before.

As he explained:

> "Through my regular visits to the Royal Marsden the treatment I had become part of and acquainted with a community of suffering – a community with whom I had little acquaintance and even less identification beforehand. When I came home after that event my wife could see that something had changed in me and with the benefit of hindsight I can confirm that as usual she was right!
>
> As I reflect on what changed in 2007 I think I can say that I fundamentally had glimpsed the horror and magnitude of

modern slavery. I'd begun to appreciate that modern slavery was a clear violation of God's created order". [59]

James' experience of vulnerability as part of a community of suffering enabled him to see others, especially the vulnerable, in a new light. He saw injustice, and resolving it became a passion for him from that point on. As a result, and in addition to his "day job" in family law, he has been actively involved in an organisation which takes on modern-day slavery legal cases – using the law to prosecute perpetrators and release victims.

Justice isn't only a value we believe in. It's a value we show our belief in with action. If someone walks past someone in need and thinks, "oh dear how sad", are they living by justice or simply theorising about justice?

Sometimes we start to get compassion fatigue and stop noticing the poor and disadvantaged around us. We can get so inwardly focused and consumed with our plans that our view of the world around us becomes very narrow and our passion for the needs of others becomes very dulled. Sometimes we need to look afresh.

As you look at the issues in society and the communities in which you live and work, what makes you say "that will not do"? What do

---

[59] Ewins, J. (19 July 2023) *Keswick Lecture*, https://www.youtube.com/watch?v=ifOXIE-5kN7Y.

Communal Value

you see and experience that plays on your mind and is lodged in your heart?

> What passion to resolve problems, bring justice and tackle harmful issues do you have and what action has that passion provoked?

There are several ways of renewing a passion for impact.

The Kingdom Test
This wider view of value goes beyond our immediate workplace or organisation we work for to the society we are impacting and the ripples of value we are creating for the common good. One approach to adding wider value in our work is to explore the idea of kingdoms – changing how we think about our work by changing the language we use to describe it.

We are used to talking about business empires, something that is taken by force and is all about control: possessing land, assets and people. Switching from talking about empire to kingdoms encourages us to look at things from a very different perspective. Kingdoms are something you serve by developing a place of safety and prosperity for everyone.

The success of an empire is measured by how much it has and can take. A kingdom's success is measured by how well its people feel and its abundance. It's the story of *The Lion King*. Scar tries to expand his empire while Mufasa and Simba nurture and support

A Life's Work

their kingdom. Under Scar, lives are destroyed as he brings only fear and scarcity. Under Simba, his kingdom flourishes with abundance and new life.

But it's not just the stuff of fairy tales. The opening words in the coronation of King Charles in Westminster Abbey were: "*I come not to be served but to serve*". The wearer of the crown is the servant of all!

We may not consider ourselves to be royalty, but we are all given responsibility, or ministry as we called it earlier, to serve within a kingdom context. Our kingdom might be a direct area of responsibility where we lead and rule or it may be a kingdom where we operate and have influence. Kingdom language helps us view the wider context within which we work and invites us to consider how we take a lead in serving the community and bringing peace and prosperity.

Kingdom language also focuses us on the current situation we are in, which might not be the spectacular success we hoped for or the strong business empire that others admire, but it is a context in which we can be of impact. The key is to understand the kingdom's values and seek not to be served but to serve the kingdom's goals.

> What kingdoms are you serving and what is your role in each? Are you serving with benevolence and building a kingdom of peace and prosperity?

Communal Value

The Valjean Test

When looking at Relational Value, we introduced the idea of grace that brings healing to relationships and acts with generosity to others wanting them to be restored and thrive in life and work. Grace not only supports relationships in the workplace but also outside work, in society, it is the power underpinning Communal Value.

The classic story of redemption has a pivot point when people are shown life-changing generosity. An unprecedented act of grace transforms an individual and underpins the way he acts in business and towards other people from that point on.

Victor Hugo's novel *Les Miserables* is an example of the transformational power of grace through the story of Jean Valjean. One act of forgiveness changes not just the course of Valjean's life, but all those he comes into contact with. Valjean had been imprisoned for 19 years for stealing bread to feed his sister's starving children. But when he receives what is meant to be freedom, he is forced to continue suffering the consequences of his sentence. His identity papers state his conviction and make him an outcast. Nobody is willing to offer him any support as a result – he is unable to get work or find anywhere to stay.

The transformational moment comes after Valjean, out of desperation, steals the silver cutlery of a bishop who had shown him kindness by giving him a meal and a bed for the night. Valjean is

A Life's Work

immediately caught by the police and brought back to the bishop's house to answer for his crime.

At this point, the bishop had several options:

- Tell the police "*that's my silver and he stole it*". Valjean would have been taken back to prison and justice would have been done – nobody would have thought this was unfair.
- Show mercy and say "*that's my silver, but he can keep it. I'm not pressing charges*". That would have been merciful and the bishop would be seen as generous and kind.

What the bishop actually chose to do went beyond mercy into grace. He said: "*keep the silver cutlery and also take the silver candlesticks*". So much silver was worth far far more than Valjean could ever earn or need in his life.

Punishing Valjean for his crimes had turned him into an outcast and – without any other option – pushed him towards stealing again. What the bishop was doing by giving so much was ensuring that Valjean would never need to steal. Rather than be an outcast he was covered with the riches of grace.

From then on, Jean Valjean lives a very different life in response to experiencing the beauty of grace. He builds a business where he treats his staff with grace and shows kindness and compassion – to the point of laying down his life for the benefit of others. The

Communal Value

bishop's forgiveness and generosity introduces Valjean to a different way of seeing people and serving people.

It's when we have that we are able to and want to live a life of redemption and generosity as well. Generosity is infectious in the workplace as favour is paid forward and recipients become transmitters.

> Have you experienced that unprecedented favour from others that releases you from something you owe or something you did that is holding you back? What would it involve for you to offer this grace to others and in what situations might you be able to offer it?

A Life's Work

The Value Conversation: David[60]
Valuable waste

What do you do when graduating with a master's from Massachusetts Institute of Technology (MIT) and with a range of high-paying jobs on offer? Move to Africa and start building toilets? That's probably not your first thought and not likely to be the most financially lucrative, but certainly exciting! Not everything that generates Communal Value is going to be obvious or glamorous by the usual definition of glamour. Sometimes it is difficult and even thankless work. Despite this, contributing value of any form is always worth the effort.

David is in the waste business and his business is definitely not a waste of time! He co-founded Sanergy, a company that processes human waste, manufactures fertiliser and produces animal feed in order to impact communities by providing sanitation where there isn't any. It has a for-profit business model and a for-social purpose.

The vision behind Sanergy began in 2009 when David Auerbach met his co-founders Lindsay Stradley and Ani Vallabhaneni at MIT. They discussed an assignment for their Development Ventures class during an orientation week hike. The challenge was to solve a poverty problem that affected at least 1 billion people.

As they walked and talked, David shared his experience of inadequate sanitation while teaching in rural China, and the others added their perspectives and reasons for this being a passion they shared in common. From that shared desire to solve a problem they all cared about, the vision driving Sanergy was born.

Sanergy is building a network of low-cost off-grid prefabricated toilets for residents of informal settlements unreached by sewer

---

60 Andrew Baughen interview with David Auerbach, 26 May 2017.

Communal Value

systems. There are three stages, each of which adds economic, social and environmental value:

- **Stage 1.** Build affordable, container-based toilets that can be located in informal settlements unreached by sewer systems. Franchise toilets to community-based operators who are trained in building their own small business.
- **Stage 2.** Collect waste from toilets deep in informal settlements using a network of handcarts to depots and trucks to processing plants. Also collect organic waste from around the city. These collections bring order to waste management, which pollutes the environment and reduces the health risk to citizens and provides a consistent source of ingredients needed in stage 3.
- **Stage 3.** Convert waste at a centralised facility into organic fertiliser, insect-based animal feed grown in high-tech pods and other products currently in development.

At each stage, Sanergy makes a financial return while simultaneously generating value through creating a wide range of new jobs and addressing serious social and economic needs.

The way the firm has grown and the decisions made are rooted in the starting story of putting entrepreneurial instinct to work to solve a social challenge. They are about building clean communities and the complex engineering to process that waste and generate a financial return is a route to the goal. David's motivations have had a clear impact on the company's strategic decisions. As David said to me:

"I'm not motivated by money so don't spend ten hours a day doing something I'm not wanting to do. I enjoy coming to work. We've built a culture where people are interested and excited. I enjoy watching people grow and I'm growing".

A Life's Work

The fascinating aspect of Sanergy is how their business decisions and impact ambitions are in sync. David is clear that he is motivated to grow the business, but his reason is to grow the impact. His ambition isn't just selling one more toilet, he's now trying to sell the model to one more city.

The ingenuity of Sanergy is in how simple offline operations and existing practices such as door to cart to truck waste collection are combined with leading-edge technology such as high protein feed production to scale an idea from one toilet to multiple cities. Behind the bright blue Fresh Life Toilets is a big team of bright minds which brings to life a whole network of logistical, technical and organisational systems.

The triple intersection of operational leadership and complex engineering to solve a social problem gives a complexity which draws together people who thrive on a big challenge and are willing to think differently. They are making a difference to people because they apply the best of their skills and resources to the greatest needs of people in a systems approach which has design thinking at its heart.

Every day I wake up is a discovery. I deal with biological processes, so I have to wait for things to change – I'm always discovering new lessons and problems to solve.

Our technology is borrowed from elsewhere and adapted for our needs such as growing larvae. We work with engineers in the USA, a company in the Netherlands and local experts.
Kennedy, R&D and Plant Manager[61]

The alchemy of Sanergy is turning shit into shillings! Solving a problem such as sanitation in informal settlements in a way which

---

[61] Andrew Baughen interview with Kennedy Michael Maobe, Engineering R&D and Plant Manager, Sanergy Farm Star plant, 4 May 2018.

doesn't create dependency on charity requires a generative attitude. The solution Sanergy has pioneered is to make money out of the waste collected so that the collection of the waste is commercially viable.

This sets up a fascinating coalition of high-tech engineering and age-old cubicle construction; large-scale processing plants and street by street toilets; high-end fertiliser products and pay-per-use toilet customers. Affordable toilets are created by turning a costly stream of waste into a revenue stream.

Sanergy's innovation is to take a systems-based approach that engages the community at every step and, in doing so, guarantees that residents of slums gain access to the hygienic sanitation services they both need and want.[62]

The legacy of Sanergy is solving a social problem with a mass market solution that is viable long term. It is easier for a startup to provide more to the "haves" of the world, but Sanergy serves the "have-nots" and makes it financially viable. The viability comes from the social benefit being produced within and throughout the value chain.

Instead of the model of selling a product to rich people and adding on something you donate to poor people (for example, sell a bottle of water and give a proportion of the profit to digging wells in Africa), Sanergy is giving to multiple people from the core of its business.

This allows Sanergy to provide Generational Value in countless forms:

- Sanitation for informal settlements.
- Providing skills to team members.
- Creating an income-generating business for operators.

---

62 Auerbach, D. (2016) *Sustainable sanitation provision in urban slums – The Sanergy Case Study.* In E.A. Thomas (ed.), *Broken pumps and promises*, Springer International Publishing Switzerland, p.212–213.

A Life's Work

- Sharing a safe place to dispose of waste.
- Cleaning rivers.
- Providing highly effective products to farmers.

The lesson for us is that impact and income don't need to be trade-offs – each of these people are discovering value for themselves by giving to others. Business is good for society when it is contributing goods that benefit society and acting for the good of people in society.

We may not be able to sell toilets for a living, but through our work we can impact the way people are living. Communal Value isn't an add-on when we start with a for-social purpose and embed that into the way we are a for-profit business. One action from this would be to put this book down for a bit and go on a hike with some inspirational friends!

Generational Value

Chapter Nine

Generational Value

Providing infrastructure, sharing expertise and building capacity for future value.
Stewarding resources, reducing threats and leaving a legacy for the next generation.

The telephoto lens looked at the Useful and Beautiful Value of what we do. The portrait lens focused on the value we develop as individuals and in relationship with others. In the last section we started looking through the wide-angle lens at Communal Value – the impact our work has in society. Now we are going to look at the other aspect of the wide-angle lens as we shift from present impact to Generational Value – the impact we generate that benefits future generations.

One of the features of value is its potential to have a long tail and keep multiplying.

- School teachers generate value in the classroom that keeps bearing fruit in children's lives and the lives of those they touch long after school's out for summer.
- Bank managers generate value by giving a family a home loan that keeps benefiting them and all who are welcomed into their home from meal to meal.
- The scientist who discovered the structure of DNA keeps benefiting society as new applications are developed and new benefits are multiplied.
- The engineers who developed computer operating systems keep bringing value to virtually every member of the population attached to a desktop, mobile or virtual device.

Generating value for the long term is a form of time travel. What we do in our work life has past, present and future perspectives. It can restore issues in the past, such as by renovating a disused building. It can generate value in the present, such as by serving people a meal. It can generate value in the future, such as by designing a cafe that serves meals to people for years to come.

In a business culture that assesses short-term gains, monitors daily performance and continually tracks achievement of goals, we can find it hard to look beyond doing what is needed right here and now. When we are able to look beyond, we see a whole pathway of value that we've helped establish.

It's the difference between selling a burger at the side of a road and actually building the road. One has immediate benefit while the other has immediate and ongoing benefit, not only in being able to drive on the road, but also in where the road takes them and what value they add from taking that journey.

The immediate benefit from selling burgers is easy to see in the cash you get and your satisfied customers. The money won't last forever though and your customers will need to eat again a few hours later. Building a road, however, has long-term ongoing value – it connects communities and makes travel and transporting goods easier. This value can be enjoyed for generations to come.

Generational Value goes beyond what we make to the legacy we leave. It is inspiring when we know that the wisdom we've passed on or the tools we've equipped others with are gifts that keep on giving. Adding value that resounds into the future is work all of us can be doing and is work worth celebrating.

A friend of mine once told me how at his school the only people with their names engraved on the wood-panelled walls of the assembly hall were Nobel Laureates and Olympic medallists. It was a high bar of entry to what was deemed a worthwhile achievement and valuable use of a life.

Such enormous pressure to achieve something so rare can become a crushing burden. But the point I have come to realise is that we can all undertake worthwhile work of lasting value by being of influence in the lives of people. By investing in the next generation, giving them wisdom, building their capacity for success and equipping them for life.

I mentioned earlier a colleague who had received a thank-you letter from a former student and just how much of an effect a simple letter had. One of the most amazing gifts is when someone tells you the impact you've had on their life – made all the more precious as most of us don't know half the impact we have had on others. Seeing how our systems, buildings and innovative solutions impact people and add value to people is a cause for great celebration.

It might have been as simple as a conversation they had with you years back that had a major effect on them and changed the direction their life then took. It might have been something you developed that enabled them to succeed in life or money you invested that opened up life opportunities for them. Learning more of how we've added is a thrill, and there is an incomparable buzz to seeing how others benefit from our work long afterwards.

In my first job as a placement student, I was asked to create a database of costs that could be used to put together estimates of expenditure on drilling and other engineering projects. The idea was to provide in one place all the costs for each item and the various charges made by suppliers, and then keep it regularly updated. This meant it could be used by any project team rather than everyone having to find every number from scratch each time. It was hard work and not the most exciting.

Generational Value

I spent hours going through invoices, but I kept going. I was clear it would be of future benefit in producing more accurate cost estimates and, therefore, more efficiently run projects. But that wasn't value I could see or fully appreciate at the time.

In fact, it wasn't until my last day of work that I realised the impact I'd had. An after-work leaving party had been organised and I was presented with a card in which many people I didn't even know had written a personal note of thanks for the database I'd created. I was so encouraged to read people's gratitude for being able to produce fast and accurate project costings long after I was gone – and the leaving party was a fun bonus! It was a good lesson for me that we do things for the benefit of others and, note to self, not always to expect a thank-you party!

The great delight in doing work that continues to be of value to others is seen in changed lives. The oft-repeated phrase is that "no one says on their deathbed, '*I wish I'd spent more time in the office*'". Value generation has that lasting-value view as well as the immediate value given. Value generators therefore care about future generations as well as quarterly financial statements.

Steps to Generational Value

As we turn towards the future, we can use the same hierarchy to study ways of generating value that lasts across the generations. Each Generational Value level looks at what we do at work, why we do it and who we do it for from a future perspective.

At the starting level, we will act for the benefit of the next generation when we realise that we have been lent the resources we have for a time by the past generations and have responsibility to pass on well.

At the middle level, we see the important role we can play in expanding the capacity for success of people. We don't just steward resources to preserve them now, but also we aim to develop resources for future benefit, equip the next generation so that they can thrive and leave behind structures and processes others can use to continue generating value.

At the deepest level, we are people who want to add value that lasts and feel we've left a legacy that can be enjoyed. Knowing that legacy is a core part of our purpose helps us to prioritise our work energies towards building that legacy and helps us celebrate the lasting joy our work is bringing to the world.

Let's look at each of these three levels in turn and explore the steps to work that builds a legacy of Generational Value for the next generation and beyond.

STEP 1:
Think as a steward

Have you ever had to house-sit for someone while they are away? I have, and I must say it made me very aware of some responsibilities knowing how much they cared about certain possessions and knowing that when they came back they'd be keen to see how I looked after things. The things in particular when I was house-sitting were pets and plants. I was very disciplined about giving the dog food and keeping him safe, and I was also very punctual in watering the plants my friend was very particular about.

I knew when the owner returned she could see from the state of her possessions just how much care I'd taken. No good giving the plants a bucket of water five minutes before my friend's key is in the latch if everything had died from dehydration two days previously – and the same goes for the dog, obviously!

When we act as a steward, we take on delegated responsibility for the owner's possessions. A steward recognises they have been given something to protect, care for and develop for a period of time.

Parents therefore are stewards of children with responsibility for their growth and wellbeing until they reach adulthood and often well beyond that! Employees are stewards of the opportunities and resources they are entrusted with. Managers and directors are stewards making decisions on behalf of the owners.

You might not have thought about your role as a steward before, but as a way of seeing the value we are producing through our work, knowing who we are producing that value for is a great help. Thinking as a steward changes how we approach our work, what responsibilities we've been given and who gave them. All work roles therefore have a stewardship element.

There are several ways of seeing value in work by thinking as a steward.

The Steward Test
To help you see how your work involves stewardship, think through the following work roles and see how the stewarding principles might apply in your situation.

- **Property Stewards.** Classically, a steward was responsible for the owner's property which involved managing an estate and/or investing assets. Crucially, the steward could care for and increase the owner's value – but not sell anything in order to profit personally or destroy the owner's value. Being a steward in this role is shown by the increase in value and the state of the property on the owner's return.

  A more modern version of this idea is a steward who manages a property. I have some very generous friends who own property and have let our family use it for a holiday. When we do, there is someone who meets us and gives us the keys, fills the fridge with basic provisions and arranges all sorts of people to upkeep the house. They don't own the house, they have delegated responsibility to steward the property and work with suppliers and contractors to sustain and develop its value. Being a steward in this case is shown in the value enjoyed by others.

  To apply this, think through what property, assets and opportunities you are responsible for in your work, who the ultimate owners are and who the other stakeholders are. How do they want you to be developing the value in your care and who do they want you to create that value for?

- **Cruise Stewards.** The term steward is also used for a staff member on a cruise liner. The passengers are there to relax and enjoy themselves, but the steward is there to work for the wellbeing of passengers. Being a steward in this role is about fulfilling allocated duties and looking to the interests of others. To apply this, think through whose wellbeing is your responsibility and what it means to be a steward serving their needs.

- **Events Stewards.** We also encounter stewards at sports games and other big events. The steward is there to ensure the safety of the ticket holders, ensure the crowd keep to the rules and act to solve problems. You can tell a steward in an incident because they're the ones running towards a problem rather than saying "it's not my problem".
To apply this, think through what dangers you are protecting others from and what problems it is your responsibility to resolve. Do you run towards a problem that is your responsibility? In what sense is that a privilege rather than a burden?

- **Financial Stewards.** Another use of steward is in the financial world when people act as a steward for investments. Being a steward in this role is shown in how much we work to the owner's time frame, vision and values. Our gain in the present is found in creating gain for the owner in the future.

To apply this, think through how you are investing for other people's futures. Who are you investing for and what future do they need?

What all these examples have in common is that they are all looking at outcomes from the perspective of others rather than ourselves. It cares about something because it cares about someone who owns it or will be using it in the future. When "it's all about you'" is the prevailing message, the steward offers a different perspective by making it all about serving others. When "I'll do what I like with my stuff" is the starting assumption, the steward offers a different perspective by making it about what the ultimate owner wants done with their stuff.

> Are we the owners who can do whatever we choose with what we have or stewards of what we have been entrusted with? If we are stewards, who are the ultimate owners?

The Next Test

Multiplying the resources we have is part of what it means to be human. We come alive when we work with what we have and make more – it's as we bring things to life that we understand our place in life. Production of goods isn't greedy or materialistic but is a natural expression of our desire to make the most of resources by developing them, increasing them, enjoying them and sharing them with others.

Generational Value

It's the last phrase – "*sharing them with others*" – that is crucial. Just because we are stewarding resources rather than owning them, a lot of the time doesn't mean we care any less about growing them, renewing them and putting them to work productively. If anything, we should care more because the value we help produce is shared with others and continues multiplying benefit into the future.

The way we use resources shows what we really think about other people we share the planet with and will hand over the planet to one day. Stewardship sees value as something bigger than ourselves and cares about how we treat the resources entrusted to us for the benefit of future generations.

It takes a willingness to look beyond our immediate needs and think about the needs of others in the future. Mark Carney, former Governor of the Bank of England, states: "*climate change is the ultimate betrayal of intergenerational equity. It imposes costs on future generations that the current generation has no direct incentives to fix*".[63] But do we only work on self-orientated incentives? Is the future of the next generation enough of a priority? We may not be directly affected but people directly related to us probably will be!

Stewards act on values of generosity. They are willing to pay now for a future they will not benefit from themselves. It's about thinking through how your work increases or decreases resources that will

---

63 Carney, M. (2021) *Value(s). Building a better world for all.* William Collins, London. p.7.

be there for others one day and seeking to leave things better than you found them. Deeply held values form vision that compels action.

Mark Carney, for example, describes how making environmental sustainability "the overarching goal" is "set by society's values of intergenerational equity and fairness".[64] When we go beyond holding resources to multiplying resources, we see the value of our work and how we are contributing to a better future.

> What values drive your present actions that have a future impact? What will future generations thank you for?

The Circle Test
Circular economy is an approach to design, manufacturing, distribution and usage of products and services that keeps the underlying resources in play for as long as possible, and then recaptures, recovers and reuses materials as far as possible. Resources go around in a circular motion rather than a linear trajectory out of the earth or into a dead-end landfill. Decoupling economic growth from resource consumption involves:

- Extending useful life and reducing speed of obsolescence.
- Reusing and repurposing.

---

64 Carney, M. (2021) *Value(s). Building a better world for all.* William Collins, London. p.249.

- Adopting smart technologies that reduce waste production and environmental impact.

As an individual, the challenge is to see how you can contribute to the circular economy when you don't have the authority to make decisions that will create systemic changes in the organisations you work for. Some ways to start that are:

- Think through your own resource stewardship responsibilities. What are you responsible for? How are you developing, replenishing and repurposing the resources available to you and what impact are your practices generating?
- Start in your local work environment with very visible and everyday changes that get everybody involved in the circular economy. Ideas include giving everyone in your workplace a reusable water bottle with branding and the ability to personalise (maybe have a "pimp my water bottle workshop" with all materials needed!) Local changes add up to a movement which can influence policies and will be more widely accepted.
- Combine education with action. Have a "lunch and learn" or lead a discussion at work on the ways we steward resources and ideas for developing a circular economy.

> What steps can you take personally to be developing and replenishing resources you are responsible for? How could you engage with others in your workplace and encourage more circular economy thinking?

STEP 2:
Add capacity

There's an old adage attributed to Chinese philosopher Lao Tzu: "*If you give a man a fish you feed him for a day, but teach him how to fish and you feed a family for a lifetime*". By extension, if you teach members of a village how to teach fishing and help them develop a fishing industry, then you feed a whole community for generations.

Generating value for future generations is often about capacity building – increasing their ability to do things, make things and develop things of value for themselves. We constantly experience the benefits of capacity building by past generations.

- Every time I drive on a straight stretch of road in England or walk under an aqueduct in Italy or look at the remains of the city wall outside my office in the City of London, I'm reminded of the Roman Empire that built them and the way their work still has impact on my daily life over a millennium later.
- Every time I enter one of the magnificent train termini in cities across the world or travel across an incredible bridge spanning a huge expanse of water, I'm reminded of the work of previous generations and how we continue to benefit from the infrastructure they built.
- Every time I use the internet to connect with other people or find information, I'm reminded of the work of software engineers and how their clever coding continues to add value to countless lives.

Generational Value

Returning to our Chinese philosophy, teaching people how to fish is one thing, but that will only continue if we build up a fishing industry that enables fishing skills to be taught, fishing boats to be built and fish to be bought and sold. Building capacity is about establishing infrastructure, platforms and codified practices that give our value-making initiatives a future dimension.

Our work has many opportunities to add capacity for value in the future as well as the present.

The Teaching Test
When looking at building value in individuals earlier in Individual Value, we looked at how teaching and mentoring develops the people we work with. In this section, we move from a portrait to a wide-angle lens and see how teaching equips a whole community of people to live lives of value.

Teaching equips people with knowledge and skill, and the capacity to be adding value. As a teacher over many years in different settings, I can testify to the joy of seeing people grow in confidence as they learn knowledge, develop skills and put theory into practice. But as we've seen already, the greatest joy comes when you see them years later still making use of what you taught and now teaching it to others.

Teaching can be about knowledge and skill, but at a deeper level it's about wisdom and the capacity to make good choices. Wisdom is knowing how to act when there are no rules we can apply. There are many decisions in life where the answer isn't written down somewhere and isn't defined in law, but is a matter of acting with wisdom. As we teach we help embed a way of thinking into society. Teaching that develops wisdom grows character and creates a more outward-looking and caring attitude towards others. We multiply value by sharing the wisdom we've been given.

But how do we add value by shaping attitudes in society? In the last chapter, we looked at Jean Valjean and how grace transformed his life. In their book *Nudge*, Thaler and Sunstein suggest that we can have a positive influence on people's behaviours and lives by adjusting the way their choices are presented to them and perceived – or providing "nudges".

These nudges can take the form of pieces of information or reminders which make the positive decision more desirable or more visible. However, providing a nudge isn't about limiting choices or control. As Thaler and Sunstein put it:

> "To count as a mere nudge, the intervention must be easy and cheap to avoid. Nudges are not mandates. Putting the fruit at eye level counts as a nudge. Banning junk food does not".[65]

---

65 Thaler, R.H. and Sunstein, C.R. (2008) *Nudge: Improving decisions about health, wealth, and happiness* London: Yale University Press, p.6.

Generational Value

For Jean Valjean, having been made an outcast for a decades-old and minor crime had actively cut decisions off. In giving Valjean the wealth and resources to live well without needing to steal, the bishop had not limited Valjean – he had freed him. Nothing was stopping Valjean from stealing again, but now it was easy for Valjean to make the choices that were actually best for him and all the people around him.

In short, Nudge Theory is about helping people to make, of their own free will, decisions that will improve their life. The information provided does not just enable an informed choice, it promotes or flags up the best choice for them. By changing choice architecture or empowering choice in the first place we have considerable opportunity to influence people, not just in what they consume day by day, but also the life choices they make into the future.

> How is your work contributing to teaching, nudging and encouraging people in wider society and how is that helping them live well for years to come?

The Infrastructure Test

Construction firms embed in a local community for a period of time as the project is completed and add value to that community by employing local workers, using local suppliers and frequenting local shops. But the larger part of the value they generate is only seen when they move off site. At this point, the building is occupied or the infrastructure (such as a new transportation or communication system) starts to operate, providing value to be enjoyed for generations.

Infrastructure makes valuable contributions to future generations by building people's capacity for success. This applies to all of our work, whether we're building houses or databases. Our involvement is often in the assets that we bring into being and the practices they enable which continue improving lives into the future. Value is in what the infrastructure enables people to create, where markets enable people to reach or who platforms enable to connect, think, solve problems and make decisions.

The ongoing value might come from establishing physical infrastructure, such as a bridge that connects one community with another, or from tech infrastructure that connects user to user. In both cases, the infrastructure is a facilitator of value – in these instances, the value of human connection. Many of the structures for retail and marketplaces that were once physical are now virtual. The building infrastructure is replaced with digital platforms but the value of enabling people to reach people is the same.

Infrastructure enables everything from education, communication, trade, travel, health and entertainment to the most fundamental of all: having a home to live in.

What ongoing value generation is your work enabling?

The Codified Test

In the world of work and business, some people are instinctively able to think strategically and some have an innate ability to think and see from a different perspective – the classic "out of the box" mentality. Others have the ability to learn from the mistakes and early wins, the dead ends and breakthroughs, and develop core principles and processes.

But then there comes a whole raft of people who don't necessarily have the instinctive skills or the knowledge from experience. There is great value in codifying principles, processes and practices in a form that others can access and benefit from over time.

Codifying might involve writing down your experience and what you learnt so that others don't need to go through the same trial and error process. It might involve establishing a way of working or system that can be adopted by others.

My experience of consulting with firms about the value they generate is that there is often considerable latent value in an organisation's corporate memory and collective knowledge. As individuals we also have skills developed and experience gained that we can usefully share with others.

This is not suggesting that the IP and trade secrets of a firm are shared without thought of the competitiveness of the organisation in the future. But it is suggesting that there may be ways of doing things that you pioneered which others could learn from and join

A Life's Work

you in using to generate ongoing value in their distinct situation. There is value in writing up the experience you've gained in your work and publishing on a platform where others can learn and create value for themselves. The bigger the gift and the wider the recipient list, the greater the value.

> What valuable insights, methods, principles and processes can you codify and share with others?

STEP 3:
Leave a legacy

In the movie *About Schmidt*, Jack Nicholson plays a recently widowed and retired insurance salesman who starts to wake up to the pointlessness of the life he's led. At the end of the film he writes a letter in his mind to a child he sponsors in Africa.

He starts by admitting that he is weak and feels like a failure. He then outlines the problem that when he dies, and he knows that won't be long, soon after everyone who knows him will also die and it will be like he never existed. He questions what difference his life has made and can't think of any. He then signs off his imaginary letter and the titles appear and the film ends.

When I watched it in the cinema, it took me all the strength I could muster not to jump out of my seat at the end. I wanted to announce from the front that nobody was allowed to leave until we'd had a chance to talk this through. I wanted to say to everyone: *"it doesn't have to be that way!"*

His conclusion that his life has made no difference is wrong. For starters, his work had Useful Value. Insurance helps people sleep at night knowing that they are covered for loss or other threats they might face, and it helps ensure others are provided for if something happens to us. He helped people live with a feeling of security and peace about the future.

Beyond this and his intrinsic Individual Value, he and his work had Communal Value. He was part of a family and had friends who he influenced, and had the opportunity to pass on to them wisdom and love that shaped them. His assumption that when those who know him die it will be as if he never existed is also wrong.

My family were glad I didn't stand up at the end of the movie but it did fuel my desire to make my legacy helping people know they all can have a valuable legacy and that nobody needs to feel their life is just a failure or meaningless. A great place to start is by redefining legacy.

What do you think about when you hear the word legacy? High on your list is probably the financial value of assets you leave to others in your last will and testament. But what if we widened the assets we valued in our legacy to include the wisdom we want to pass on and the memories we want others to keep hold of?

A Life's Work

In business circles, legacy can have negative connotations about being an old "legacy system" that is being retired and stopped. But what if the legacy of our work was in the vision and enabling we catalyse that is being lived?

When people read obituaries and it says how much they left behind, the answer that is common to all is "everything". But what is the "everything" you will leave behind? What gifts will you leave with the next generation that will help them live and pass on to the generation after them?

As another movie, *Gladiator*, puts it: "*what we do in this life echoes into eternity*". Our actions influence people who influence people and so on. There's a real delight in seeing others you've worked with applying what they learnt from you in their future careers or children you've taught then teaching the same thing to their children.

I think of Simon who worked in my team as an apprentice minister and is now running a very creative church community in North London. I think of my daughter Charlotte who got the bug for walking holidays in Switzerland and is now taking her own children to the same campsite.

All work can leave a legacy and there are several ways of clarifying and celebrating that.

Generational Value

The Letter Test
Great wills don't just say what the deceased left to whom, but also why. When we know the intention behind our gift we give with much more joy. It's the difference between transferring cash to someone for a birthday gift and buying something they will treasure long after their birthday. Our gift has intention and we have the joy of knowing the value we've been able to bestow on someone we value.

But could these principles be applied in the workplace? An immediate application would be to your parting gift when you leave a job role or place of employment. Do we just leave a note saying: "*all the budget is spent and there's nothing left for you. Good luck!*"? Or do we leave a work version of a last will and testament that outlines what we've developed, what opportunities we've invested in and what hopes we have for those who take the next steps?

A leaving letter needn't be self-promoting or overly directive. It's more of a guide to the treasures you've worked on and want them to enjoy, and it's an expression of the future intentions behind our past and present actions. It can therefore be written in our head long before we actually leave as a way of ensuring we keep a focus on the next generation and the value of legacy.

> What would your letter say?

Returning to the cinema, my work is done if there are no more Warren Schmidts out there thinking their work counts for nothing and they will soon be forgotten!

A Life's Work

The Leaf Test

One of the exciting aspects of the legacy you leave behind is that what you had planned is often only a partial picture of the value it becomes. The activities we pour ourselves into end up forming part of a greater whole.

J.R.R. Tolkien wrote a short story, called *Leaf by Niggle*,[66] to remind himself that even if his *The Lord of the Rings* trilogy remained unfinished and read by very few people (not a worry that was founded as it turned out), his role was to work on something much bigger and more lasting than he could yet imagine.

Niggle was a painter who, true to his name, would obsess about the details and lose sight of the more important issues of life. Niggle had a dream of painting a leaf and then a tree and then a whole land of forests and mountains that opened out. He therefore got a huge canvas and began painting. But because he was better at painting leaves than landscapes he concentrated on getting some of the leaves done.

As time went on, he got distracted by his kind heart and helping other people with their problems so that he didn't get very far with the painting and then caught a chill and fever. As he lay close to death, he was desperately sad that his work remained so unfinished.

---

66 J.R.R. Tolkien **Leaf by Niggle** was first published in the Dublin Review in January 1945. The story can be found in Tolkien, J.R.R. (2009) **Tree and leaf: including MYTHOPOEIA**. HarperCollins, London.

After his death, the people who bought his house discovered the unfinished canvas, which by then had deteriorated, and only one beautiful leaf remained intact. It was removed to a museum where it was displayed as "Leaf: by Niggle" and was seen by a very few as it was placed in a dark corner.

But that's not where the story ends for Niggle, who passes from death to the afterlife and starts a new life in a world where all is made new. One day in this new world, he goes on a trip to the countryside and notices his tree is there in reality within a forest. To his delight he sees that all the leaves are in place. He left with just a few leaves created and now it is finished and perfect.

The story contains a warning to get on with your leaf rather than constantly being distracted. It's also an encouragement that your leaf is part of something bigger. We get our work in context when we see the bigger picture it fits into. Tolkien wrote the story to remind himself of the perfect reality that his work expresses and contributes to.

He saw his work as leaves which are connected to the trees of a forest that is part of eternal reality. Informed by Christian teaching, he believed that one day we will go to a new earth where the value we worked to produce will be displayed in the perfection we then live in and the people we then live with.

Whether or not you share that belief with him, it is true for all of us that we have beautiful work to focus on as acts of kindness to show along the way which contribute to something far bigger than us and probably far more long-lasting than us.

> What's "your leaf", as it were, that is the priority and legacy of your work? How does the work you do now contribute to something bigger? What are you adding that is enabling the story to continue and value to develop?

Generational Value

The Value Conversation: Helen[67]
Value is found in many different places

As a teacher, it's hard to forget the power of legacy. Helen is an experienced teacher who is now training future teachers – she is deeply aware of the power of Generational Value. She described to me how her university building is in an area of London with many social challenges, and yet the gleaming towers of global bank headquarters are within eyesight.

She wonders to herself what the bankers think of the value created in the small university campus that they look down on from their executive suites. As we talked, I was struck by how clear Helen was about the value she was generating and how refreshing that was compared to many bankers I've met who know the value of a trade better than the value of life.

For Helen, one of the big influences on her attitude to work and the value of others was going with her dad, who ran a bus company, after school on some of his site visits. Together they would visit bus depots.

Helen observed the Relational Value he generated as he went straight to the garage, rather than the office, and spoke to the engineers mending engines and staff cleaning vehicles. He would talk to them individually and thank them by describing how valuable what they were doing was to the purpose of the company in transporting people and to the ability of others in the company to do their job.

Their success as a bus company was built on the loyalty of customers which was reliant on the reliability of the vehicles and fostered by the cleanliness of the interiors. Helen knew that, for her dad, talking to staff wasn't a management technique, but a heartfelt understanding

---

[67] Interview by Andrew Baughen with Helen Jones 14 October 2021.

that they were a team of people who were enabling other people to travel to their work and meet with their friends.

They had good purpose and it was everybody's business to achieve that well.

Helen's formative trips with her dad stayed with her when she went into teaching. She made a point of talking to as many students as she could each day and finding out about their lives rather than just being interested in their grades. She now continues to multiply the value teachers can have on children's lives by teaching students to be teachers.

She described to me how much she cares that the students are trained well because "they are going to be let loose on children and I care that those children are given the best chances in life by teachers who get the value they have the potential to give".

For Helen, teaching isn't just about information download, but also about shaping the character and maturity of the next generation:

"At times I have felt frustration and pressure to increase school results at any cost. Whilst I have always advocated raising standards, I have always held a firm belief that the data was not the be all and end all of the success of a school.

For me, it was more about looking beyond the data and knowing what needed to be done to ensure that children developed a sense that success was also found in their ability to be kind, serve others and be the best they could be in whatever job they aspired to do".

One example she gave was of a student saying to her after a lecture "great sesh miss". Rather than politely saying "thanks" and moving swiftly on, Helen asked her to come over. She explained that her name was Helen and that "sesh" isn't a real word. So she asked the student to say the sentence again.

Generational Value

With a smile on her face the student said, "Great lecture Helen, thank you", to which Helen replied: "thank you [name] for your valuable contributions today, I appreciate your engagement in the material".

It may be a small point, but when they add up, they are all about investing in teachers who will multiply value to future generations of students and, in turn, shape them for life. Many types of value are being generated in the university and also in the bank headquarters that share the same city.

Helen is impacting the lives of the future workforces of office buildings. She is building Generational Value so people can lead lives of Useful Value. Both are valuable and both are necessary to the health and prosperity of the city.

Value for Life

Chapter Ten

Value for Life

Knowing who you are.
Living what you're here for.
Enjoying where you're going.

Imagine you have to recruit a colleague to join your project team. You will be working closely together for an extended period of time and will need to rely on each other in order to achieve your goals. What factors are most important to you when making your selection from a list of potential candidates? Is it just about competency and having the best skills for the work, or do you also value depth of character and work attitudes? What about chemistry – do you take account of how you feel when they walk in the room?

Competency, character and chemistry are all necessary when we are thinking about working with others, and are also all vital when others are thinking about working with us! As well as doing, we are thinking and feeling people.

When we turn up on a Monday morning we bring our body, mind and spirit with us. Human flourishing is a big topic in the business world and there's a growing recognition that thriving at work involves caring for the whole person: physical, emotional and spiritual.

This book has looked at lots of ways of generating value in our work. We've explored each type of value at a practical starting level, a relational heart level and then a deeper level that gets to the soul of the matter. This third level gets to the core of the issue and, for me, is rooted in my personal beliefs, which shape what I see as important, and therefore give meaning to my work and significance to my life.

For many of us, faith in something or someone greater than ourselves shapes the way we see the world, work in the world and add value to the world. As a result, what we believe in has been embedded into the way business has been done for centuries in diverse cultures and contexts across the world.

We are doing, thinking, feeling and believing people. What we have faith in to provide meaning and value in work and life makes a difference in practice – our doing is connected to our believing.

> Do you engage your heart and soul at work and, if so, what is the state of your heart and soul?

As we draw to a conclusion there is value in affirming the beliefs behind the actions. A grand symphony has a final movement that recapitulates the themes and brings them together in music that touches the soul.

In the same way, this final section gives the opportunity to do what could be described as "soul care", and review some of the deep truths behind the value we generate, and some of the foundational principles therefore to adding value from a heart that is full and a soul that is healthy.

I warmly invite you to engage in some heart and soul care based on three deep truths we can know for ourselves:

- I know who I am.
- I know what I'm here for.
- I know where I'm going.

Each deep truth leads to a foundational principle. Practising these with your heart and mind will transform your attitudes and actions at work in ways that are good for the soul.

BELIEF 1:
I know who I am

There's a chant from the terraces at a football match directed towards the opposing team which asks the simple question, "who are you?" And when each player is announced, the home side supporters shout "who?" The reality is they know full well the answer to their questions but are taunting people with a different colour shirt that they are nobody.

Judging from how many fans wear the uniform of their team and sing the anthems along with other fans, it means a lot to belong. Knowing who we are and where we belong defines how we watch the match and whether we cheer or sigh when a goal is scored. In the same way, knowing who we are and where we belong shapes our attitudes to work and our actions at work.

When people introduce me to others, I can tell immediately what they value about me or think the person receiving the introduction will find valuable to know. If they think my value is in the family I'm part of, the introduction will focus on my background, who I'm related to or where I was brought up.

If they think my value is in who I know and who else values me, the focus might be on the friends I have or the networks I am part of. But more often than not, the focus is on what I do, my work and position in my career, because they think that what I do and the success I have achieved is the clearest measure of my value in the world.

But it's a trap. We saw that when we studied Individual Value earlier on and contrasted Positive Charlie's belief in intrinsic value that doesn't have to be earnt with the attitude of Negative Charlie who has less confidence in his worth, which he feels is assigned based on his performance.

Being valued only for what you do represents a very real and present danger that traps you in an endless cycle, forcing you to keep performing. After all, if I'm only valued for a piece of work then I'm only valued if I keep producing that work. This makes our value conditional on continual assessment and is dependent on present performance continuing in the future.

When we reduce the value of who we are and our work to a simple list of things we do, it reduces what it means to be a human being. It traps us in a fragile dependency on performance ratings and a fear of not continuing to be good enough to earn the value of others.

I'm aware of the potential conflict of messaging here and anticipate the question "isn't the whole of this book about doing things of value?" Yes, it is. But I hope that the encouragement to be of value has never implied that we do that to earn our value as human beings, and has always started from the assumption that we are of ultimate value already.

One of the ironies of knowing who I am is that I can then turn the focus from myself to others and live life. Self-forgetfulness is the way to happiness, because rather than trying all the time to prove myself or repair myself, I can live life in the light of knowing myself. It's a bit like having a painful foot that you think about every time

A Life's Work

you walk and become constantly cautious about, and yet you don't think about it at all when it's working fine.

Which brings us to the first foundation principle that is good for our soul:

FOUNDATION PRINCIPLE 1
We can only give from what we've received.

There's a big difference between going into a room of people who love you and are rooting for you and going into a room full of strangers you have to prove yourself to. Our whole demeanour changes when we feel secure and can act with confidence.

The more I know that I'm valued, why I'm valued and what it means to have ultimate worth, the more I live from an abundance of value. I can also enjoy the particular skills developed in me, the resources shared with me and the work entrusted to me as opportunities to give from what I have been given.

Knowing I'm loved means I don't need to search for love from others but can love out of compassion and fullness, not expecting anything in return. I'm not trying to prove myself because I'm approved of.

> Do you know that pre-approval? Are you only valued by what you do or do you do what you do because you are already valued?

Value for Life

BELIEF 2:
I know what I'm here for

I've been to many graduation ceremonies in my lifetime and could probably give lots of opinions on what makes a good graduation speech, but that is another book! Although I've been to lots of ceremonies, which are quite similar in format, my reason for going and my engagement with the proceedings has been radically different over time.

The first ceremony I ever went to was as a student. I was receiving my undergraduate degree and family were there in the audience to cheer me on as I walked across the stage and received my certificate. Fast forward several decades and I'd switched seats – now I was the family cheering on my daughter as she walked across a stage and received her certificate.

These days, my place has changed again and I'm sitting on a stage applauding students I taught receiving their degrees. Same activity, different identity. Same celebrations, different motivations. Knowing who we are leads us to know why we're here and what role we have.

I went from gaining Individual Value as a student to generating Generational Value as the parent investing in my children, and then to celebrating the Useful Value given to the students I had taught and the Communal Value they would now be offering society. The more we know our purpose behind the things we do, the more we will value the things we do.

Which brings us to the second foundation principle that is good for our soul:

FOUNDATION PRINCIPLE 2
We all have purpose but not all purposes have equal value.

Our world is a place of purpose. As we've seen, value isn't just hanging from a tree ready for us to grasp – even the fruit of the tree needs cultivating, watering and harvesting. All people have a role in generating value and nobody should feel that they can sit on a deckchair all day being served.

Throughout this book we have celebrated the great gift of work is that it gives us the opportunity to contribute to the world, adding value by investing our time and talents in something useful, producing what is beautiful and having an impact on the lives of others in our workplace, in wider society and in future generations.

Purpose is part of how we're made and having purpose is what fuels how we live. But not all purposes are of equal value. There are four contrasting purposes we can have at work based on the four attitudes to value we outlined at the start: Value Guard, Value Grab, Value Give-away and Value Generate.

Survival – *"Work is a grind"*

The main objective in this view of work is to do as little as possible in order to survive. It sees work as an ultimately futile grind that has to be done to earn enough to eat and live, but life is seen as starting when we leave work at 5pm or get a holiday from work. This shapes an indifference to value that is self-orientated with minimal expectations until work is finished and "real life" begins.

Success – *"Work is a game"*

When work is seen as a game, there are winners and losers: the objective is to win as big an amount of value for yourself as possible. The assumption is that there is a scarcity of value so that I need to fight to get my share. This shapes a competitive attitude where my purpose is to secure resources, build advantage, beat the competition and win at all costs. I treat work therefore like a military campaign and treat people as dispensable pawns in my plans to conquer.

Significance – *"Work is a goal"*

This view of work makes achieving significance your purpose, with a goal of making your mark on the world. It's an attitude historically associated with people working for charities and not for profits, where the value is in good works rather than cash mountains. But doing good in business has gone mainstream and the desire for significance is fuelled by a desire to gain social media likes and boost our social status.

Service – *"Work is a gift"*

When we see work as a gift, our purpose is to serve and make the most of the opportunities we receive. We work because we are part of a business ecosystem where we add value and receive value at the same time. Seeing our purpose in service is an orientation of the heart that celebrates opportunity and accepts responsibility to steward the resources and opportunities we have been given and shapes a view of abundance in business.

There are contrasting types of purpose, but not all will feed our soul. We need to be clear therefore what purpose gets us out of bed in the morning and know whether our purpose is purely financial, coldly transactional or inclusively soulful.

> Do you get out of bed just because you need to do certain activities or because the day is calling you and there's a whole lot of value for you to create and celebrate?

BELIEF 3:
I know where I'm going

The great stories are ones that open up new worlds for us to imagine and enjoy as we go on a journey through that world and to a destination. Novels such as *The Lord of The Rings* are about a journey which brings anticipation, sometimes peril and often challenges. But we keep reading, and the actors in the story keep going because of the end, even when it's far from sight, and we are glad when the journey is complete and there is the safety of home.

Where that destination is will fundamentally affect how we go on the journey and how we feel about completing the journey. If the destination is sadness and scarcity we will go on the way with reluctance and increasing concern as the end gets closer. At the most extreme, it's being in a cell awaiting execution.

But if the destination is happiness we will go on the way with energy and building anticipation as what we are looking forward to comes nearer. It's the first sight of the sea in the distance when we go on holiday or the home we are longing to get back to where family are there to greet us and celebrate with us.

One of the complications to this is that we can take the same journey as others, but have very different experiences on the way depending on our expectation of what awaits us at the end.

It's the difference between taking a train to Cambridge to have a difficult conversation about a relationship crisis and taking the same train to attend a delightful dinner at one of the colleges. It's the difference between me driving to a hospital to visit a friend who was dying and making the same drive to the hospital with my wife as she was in labour with our first child.

Which brings us to the third foundation principle that is good for our soul:

FOUNDATION PRINCIPLE 3
We enjoy a journey more when there's joy at the destination.

We care about the pain and wrong we see around us because we know that falls far short of what the Earth could be, and for many of us what we think the Earth should be. We work now in hope, looking to a better day coming. Hope gives us endurance as we fix our eyes on home.

That was the dream at the core of Martin Luther King's famous speech – the day when he will be home at last when prejudice and hatred is no longer. And yet he also knew the work he was commissioned for in the meantime.

Knowing where I'm going changes my attitude to what I'm now doing. For me personally, that's why the *Seek lasting treasure* and *Leave a legacy* steps of this book are so important. My life's purpose is to invest in treasure that will last. It's shaped by *The Parable of the Shrewd Manager* from the Gospel of Luke.[68]

This is a story about a manager who is just about to get fired from his job, so he decides to call in all the creditors that he managed on behalf of the business owner. He then informs them that he has cut

---
68 Luke 16:1-15.

their invoices so that they don't need to pay back so much interest anymore on their debts. He is commended for this because it shows he was more interested in building friendships, which will last after his job is gone, than building up his profits which will soon run dry.

The lesson is that our worldly wealth won't last forever, therefore it is better to invest in authentic lasting treasure rather than the counterfeit treasure of a full bank account. The friendship and positive impact we make on the world will be something we can enjoy long after our worldly wealth has gone.

This parable has always inspired me to focus my life decisions around the principle of investing in lasting value – eternal treasure that is about people I will enjoy friendship with in this world and the next. That's my purpose in writing this book.

This is one small way of helping you, dear reader, see more of the room of jewels – the wide range of treasure you can enjoy and invest your life in. The more we see the array of value and know who we are and where we're going, the more we will invest wisely and generate value that brings us joy and gives us purpose.

This book has been all about seeing value more clearly. It's like taking a hike into the mountains and glimpsing the view as you turn each corner. The higher you go, the more of the view you see, and as you get above the tree-line you see the full picture. Many times, I've had that experience on a mountain walk of taking a photo and then five minutes later seeing a better view and taking another photo, and so I go on till I have the perfect photo to treasure.

I hope you've had that experience reading this, and that you now have an exciting, inspiring and full picture of the Whole Value you are generating and have the potential to generate. My dream is that this restored view of value will inspire you that you are inherently valuable and motivate you to generate lasting value that people believe in for the benefit and wellbeing of generations to come.

Please be in touch with me via the soulfulenterprise.org website if you'd like to ask questions, enquire about Whole Value workshops or hear about more ways you can keep exploring the themes of this book and work with heart and soul.

About the author

Andrew Baughen studied business finance as an undergraduate at City of London Polytechnic and began his career at Coopers & Lybrand where he was a management consultant specialising in banking strategy. He then studied theology and became the Vicar of Saint James Clerkenwell where he started the School of Faith. He has written two books on strategy and completed an Executive MBA programme at Bayes Business School (formerly Cass).

Andrew continues to work in the "theotech" sector at the intersection of business and theology. He is currently researching the difference between soul-full and soul-less organisations and how worldview shapes the way we see our work and make ethical decisions. He has created a tool that maps the wide range of value generated by a business (wholevalue.org) and writes about the wider value of our work and how our view of the world shapes the way we live and work in the world (soulfulenterprise.org).

He is an Honorary Visiting Fellow and a Visiting Lecturer at Bayes Business School. He lectures on business ethics and is currently developing a series of Soul Factor talks by business leaders exploring how they work with heart, mind and soul (soulfactor.org).

Andrew is married to Rachel, and they have two daughters and two granddaughters. He enjoys cycling, photography and saying "yes please!" to eating dessert.

Printed in Great Britain
by Amazon